# DRIVEN BY F.I.R.E.

## Ignite the Flames of Success Through

## Faith, Intensity, Re-Invention and Enthusiasm

## Louie Herron

First Printing

Published by
Southern Lion Books
Historical Publications
1070 Jordan Road
Madison, GA 30650

www.southernlionbooks.com

Manufactured in the United States of America.

ISBN: 978-48358-791-2


Library of Congress Control Number: 2016951252

The paper in this book meets the guidelines for permanence and durability of the Committee on Production Guidelines for Book Longevity of the Council on Library Resources.

# ACKNOWLEDGEMENTS

Writing this book has been a true adventure and accomplishment in my life. This milestone has some irony.

First, I was terrible in English, grammar, literature or any form of communicating on paper. Secondly, my mother always talked about writing a book, but passed away before it was ever accomplished. So Mom! Here ya go.

I want to thank Sandy for always pushing me in many different ways. She is brilliant and extremely competent in many areas. Her direction was not always accepted, but she was consistently correct (imagine that). Thank you Sandy for all you do, and I love you very much.

To my daughter, Mackenzie and my son LJ, I love you guys and I'm so grateful to be your father daily. Let this be a testament that regardless of who tells you that "you can't" in life, it's possible!

I also would like to thank Mike Jones with Discover Leadership Training for truly inspiring me in 2002 to think beyond my perspective. To be the wind not the flag. To understand the difference from being committed vs. interested. Lastly, understanding that every day is a great day to be alive!

This book is dedicated to Mackenzie Herron and LJ Herron. Through unbelievable faith, ridiculous intensity, taking the time to re-invent yourself and having enthusiasm that would illuminate a room, they can accomplish anything.

# INSPIRATION / THANK YOU
## Dr. Eric Thomas

In 2010, I was running on a treadmill in Milledgeville, GA at the local Bodyplex Gym. As usual, I was listening to a podcast or YouTube video of pastors, motivational speakers, or sports. I turned on, at the time, a video of an unrecognizable, but soon to be discovered, talent, E.T. the "hip hop preacher." He was one of my favorites (and still is), and now one of, if not the #1, motivational/inspirational communicators on the planet.

In this video he was talking about his "story" and how he was writing his first book called "Secrets to Success." At that moment, I said to myself if E.T. can write a book, I can write a book!

From that video that day, this book was born. Then of course doubt crept in. How can you write a book? You were terrible in school, and then dropped out of college.

Overcoming those thoughts (as we all face daily), I create "Driven by F.I.R.E." I want to give E.T a huge 'Thank You' a shout-out, because I can honestly say I don't believe this bo would have been written if it were not for that day. Since th time I have had a chance to meet Eric and express my gra tude for his work and contribution to people all over the wo

Thanks again E.T.

# TABLE OF CONTENTS

# FOREWORD

This book reminded me how much of an impact I have on people. The success that Louie has experienced also speaks to that impact. I know on some level my teaching, training and coaching with Louie has prepared him to create this masterpiece blueprint for your personal success.

As a young man growing up in the projects in Houston, Texas, my role model was a herculean mother who worked her fingers to the bones and demonstrated for me what it meant to play full-out. The result of her hard work was me successfully pursuing my dream to be a commercial pilot, which opened doors I had not imagined.

I later created a program focused on teaching high school students the value of focusing on what they wanted and accepting 100% personal responsibility to make it happen. I showed them the value of continually changing their approach, focused on their outcome, never blaming and never allowing quitting to be an option.

This Soul Patrol became so popular that it was featured on most of the national news programs, magazines and talk shows. The program received significant recognition from Presidents Bush and Clinton. The program went national and was presented to nearly 4 million teenagers.

Now as a successful author and businessman, I continue to give this gift that God gave me through Discover Leadership Training. My focus is to inspire, motivate and empower others to take control of their lives and never blame another person or circumstance for what they have not accomplished.

There is a significant opportunity for you to benefit from this book. It is critical that you get out of your personal comfort zone in order for you to gain those benefits.

I suggest that as you read this potentially life changing book that you understand that this is not directing you to focus on what's wrong, what's broken or what needs to be fixed.

The real power available to you through Louie's personal story is that you can take what you may have perceived as bad and use it to drive you forward to a positive outcome.

The critical awareness is you must identify the positive outcome you are committed to achieve. As Louie so eloquently states in his book "struggles don't happen to you, they happen for you." I trust that once you have completed this book you will realize that your struggles are gifts to be celebrated.

The excuses and blaming can stop today. You can begin a powerful, courageous life today, because one of the greatest gifts each of us have been given is the gift of choice. Knowing that you can choose to believe anything that you want to believe, why not choose to believe in yourself? This book will have a positive impact on your life.

Mike Jones

# DRIVEN BY F.I.R.E.

**Ignite the Flames of Success Through**

**Faith, Intensity, Re-Invention and Enthusiasm**

# DRIVEN BY F.I.R.E.

# INTRODUCTION, OR LIFE'S OWNER'S MANUAL

We've all had those moments where we didn't know what to do. All we knew is what we were doing wasn't working and no matter how hard we tried, we couldn't figure things out.

We've all struggled. We've all felt beaten down and frustrated. If only life came with an owner's manual – a detailed one. If only you could turn to a page when you needed help and you would know exactly what to do next.

Admit it: you've felt like giving up. You've struggled with your life in some way and you've thought to yourself (maybe quietly) that you just couldn't do it anymore. You're not the only one.

But it doesn't have to be that way. You can make it through, even if you have no idea what 'it' looks like on the other side.

Experience has taught me that no matter who or where we are in life, we will, at some point, come upon challenging circumstances. We all have relational, professional, financial, spiritual, emotional or even physical issues.

We all have struggles, even those who seem to have things together struggle during their lives. To overcome these struggles and reach success, you must learn how to handle the times when things aren't going your way.

## YOU'RE NOT ALONE

Let's look at one of the most respected men in American history. By the age of fifty, he had experienced disappointment after disappointment.

He was forced out of his home, along with his family, at age seven, and his mother died two years later.

At twenty-two, he lost his job as a store clerk. He wanted to go to law school, but because of his impoverished childhood he couldn't get past the admissions process. He also lost a young love to an untimely death.

At twenty-eight, he was rejected when he asked his next love to marry him. He failed in his first two bids for Congress, and when elected on his third attempt, lost his re-election two years later.

He suffered a nervous breakdown, lost a young son, and made two unsuccessful runs for a seat in the US Senate. Can you imagine? Most people would have given up completely after just a few disappointments.

But not this man.

After all of these adversities, at the age of fifty-one, Abraham Lincoln was elected the 16th President of the United States.

What can Lincoln's life teach us? What lessons can each of us learn from his dispiriting life experiences? Struggles don't happen to you, they happen for you.

Great success and the respect of others don't simply happen. As with Lincoln, a life of integrity and a life worth admiring can only occur after struggle.

# WHAT I KNOW

I know a thing or two about this. My biological father disappeared after he divorced my alcoholic mother when I was three. She re-married a man who was a strict disciplinarian.

I've been fired four times and demoted twice. I've had my life savings embezzled. I've spent more holidays alone than

I care to count. I've had many a year with multiple W-2s. I've had to "buy back" multiple car transactions that cost over a half million dollars due to a fraud ring that nearly crippled my business. I've been divorced (one of my worst experiences EVER).

And I know I'm not special.

So, when does change happen? When does a person figure things out and move forward, despite all of the things that seem to be telling them to turn back and give up?

You don't need to know exactly what this means right now, you already have sensed it: ***information changes situations***. The more you know, the more you can change.

This is probably why you were motivated to pick up this book in the first place – you know you needed to learn more in order to get more from your life.

In this book we will key in on four main drivers of success: ***Faith, Intensity, Re-invention, and Enthusiasm***. We will also learn the principles of purpose, vision, renewing your mind, goals, and becoming outcome-focused. These principles are the **seeds** we will plant to create the garden of opportunities for your successes. While there are many in our world who understand these principles, there are far too many who still believe in a different kind of luck. L.U.C.K— in my words, "Laboring Under Correct Knowledge."

***Striving for success without hard work is like trying to harvest where you haven't planted.***

As you read this book, it's time to ask the Lord to strengthen your back, not lighten your load. (James 1:2)

**"Dear brother and sisters, WHENEVER trouble comes your way, let it be an opportunity for joy"**

## DRIVEN BY F.I.R.E.

How do you have joy in the midst of pain, struggle, setback and turn it into success? Well, hang on, because you've found the right book to experience the F.I.R.E.

I truly hope you are inspired and motivated to achieve your goals and live your dreams.

# 1 - START YOUR ENGINE(S)

I don't know about you, but I know I'm not the most energetic person first thing in the morning. Even though I know how many things I have to do and I know what I need to accomplish, I may take my time getting out of bed.

For many readers, I'm sure that life has felt much the same way. You may have felt as though you've been asleep for years. Even though you may have realized this, it doesn't mean it's easy to wake up and start on your new life.

Or is it?

By thinking about how you can start your engines right now, you can begin to change not only the direction of your life, but also the direction of your impact in the world.

## <u>READY? SET. GO!</u>

> *"All scripture is God-breathed and is useful for teaching, rebuking, correcting, and training in righteousness. So that the man of God may be toughly equipped for every good work." ~ 2 Timothy 3:16-17*

You're here for some reason. Maybe you know what that reason is – or maybe you don't.

Maybe you want to better your life, whether this means you graduate from high school or college, become an entrepreneur, learn from someone who has had some troubles and trials, gain more knowledge, or work toward whatever is important to you right now.

You can have the things you want if you are willing to learn the principles and get started now – not tomorrow, not next week. When you are done with this book, you will have no more excuses.

What you will have is a solid path to take your life to the next level.

It's time to stop hitting the snooze button on your life. It's time to get out the key and start your own engine.

And the good news is that you're not the first person to take this step. You already knew that you needed to find a key, and why is that?

Because success leaves clues for everyone. Even you.

You're not the first person to become a success, even if they didn't know the way. You're not the first person to explore their own definition of success.

You also won't be the last.

Every great journey begins with one step and it begins with moving forward, turning on the engine, and shifting into the right gear at the right time. Remember, going through pain is temporary and it will subside, but quitting on the other hand lasts forever.

# <u>START WITH A SOLID FOUNDATION</u>

*"Now faith is the substance of things hoped for, the evidence of things not seen." ~ Hebrews 11:1*

Everything begins at the beginning, and quite often the beginning begins when you shift your mind in a new direction. My shift came when I realized that life doesn't happen to you, it happens for you.

Let's move back to my life so you can get to know me better. My mother divorced my biological father when I was three years old.

She remarried when I was five and my stepdad became my new father figure. He became a huge influence on my life, but he was also old school, and bulldog-tough to everyone.

I could go into detail about what 'tough love' looked like to him, but I think you can read between the lines. Here is what I will say, he was (and still is) a generous man, but not without a price. This created constant tension between my mother and stepdad and made my home life a continuous struggle.

My mom was a loving person and always tried to protect me from my dad's wrath, but she had her parenting flaws too.

Because of this, I just wanted out of the house.

I wanted out of the house because I didn't want my environment to hold me back. To this day, I firmly believe that while you might have a strained upbringing, you can learn from the people who raised you.

No matter what, you need to start with a solid foundation, even if you're the one that has to build it.

# WHAT I KNEW

My dad worked harder than the average man, and he prospered because of it. He took over his parents' roofing company in south Florida, grew the business, and made more money than he could count.

He dabbled in other businesses and gambled big dollars and did so regularly. He was an entrepreneur and a huge risk-taker with a No-Fear spirit. He won some, and lost some, went bankrupt, then made it all again and then went bankrupt again. What he never did was stop trying!

I believe that watching this was when one of the first seeds of my entrepreneurial spirit was planted. He worked hard, and expected the kids to work too. Sleeping in was not allowed, as dad always said that sleep was for broke people.

At a young age, I knew I wanted more from my life. I knew that I wanted a different life, and that meant I looked to others for guidance. It began when my grandparents, who were both outspoken Christians, talked my mom into putting me into a Christian school in sixth grade. Hollywood Christian School was the beginning of my faith in Christ.

I began to understand that if you want to change, you can change. You can learn from what you know and move forward anyway. The only one that could ever hold me back was ME.

People tend to blame their circumstances or environment for what they achieve or don't achieve. But when you walk by faith and not by sight, you can't blame your circumstances, because faith overcomes every circumstance.

So what is faith? It is the ability to see in the darkness what your creator has already shown you in the light. A high level of faith gives you certainty, yet when you are certain about something, there is no room for faith.

When there is a high level of faith, the by-products are passion and obsession. Passion and obsession together give you the desire you need to achieve your goals. A goal without Faith is just a wish.

## MANUFACTURER RECOMMENDATIONS

At the end of every chapter, you will see "Manufacturer Recommendations" for you to use. It's a little like homework, and it's going to help you focus what you learned into action.

So grab a notepad, a pen, and a highlighter. This is about your life and where you want it to go.

## #1 - Success Leaves Clues

Choose five people to interview. They may be people already in your life or others you would like to know who, in your eyes, have achieved success. List them here.

Set aside a time to interview with all five people. Your goal is to gain information from them so as to empower yourself. For example, "Name the three things you did to influence your mindset about success," or "If you had to do it all over again what would you have changed and why?" Stay away from yes/no response type questions because you are looking for detailed information in the answers. After all, information changes situations.

Create interview questions before your interviews and take this step seriously. Remember, these people have paved the road. They have made the mistakes and achieved the victories from which you can learn. Try using the same list of questions for all the interviews. You will find common themes in their answers.

Possible categories you might use to focus your questions are:

- Financial

- Spiritual

- Physical

- Health

- Relationships

## #2 - Identify Your Why

Your 'why' is that which inspires you.

What inspires you? What image or possession that you desire comes to mind?

List three 'why's' in your life that fuel your ambition.

# DRIVEN BY F.I.R.E.

List each "why". Explain how it motivates you.

1 _____

2 _____

3 _____

Make a decision right now that you will work towards being grateful for all circumstances in your life now and in the future, good or bad!

## #3 – Affirm Yourself

I understand that everything in my life (good/bad) happens for a Divine reason. I will accept the concept that things in life don't happen to me but they happen through me or for me. No longer will I complain about circumstances, because I realize that circumstances happen to all people. I realize it's not what happens to me but how I interpret it, as well as handle it. Bad things happen to all people, and it's always to make me stronger and to develop character for my own good. I _____ am committed to moving forward toward my outcome.

# 2 - NAVIGATION SYSTEMS

*"For we walk by faith, not by sight."* ~ 2 Corinthians 5:7

Even though we might look like we know what we're doing (to everyone but ourselves), it's not uncommon to feel completely lost, completely alone, and completely without direction.

It's called, well, life.

Life is a journey that doesn't come with a map and it doesn't come with a way to figure it out. The only way you learn about your life and its direction is by choosing a way to turn or a way to turn around.

You are the navigator, and while God will guide you too, you need to be willing, able, and ready to go somewhere. (Noah didn't build the ark from the couch talking about it.)

Being stuck is not what you need right now – and saying that you don't want to go anywhere because you don't know the way...well, that isn't going to take you far either.

## **FINDING YOUR COURSE**

After my sixth grade year of school, my personal perspective of life changed completely. It was in the sixth grade that I accepted the Lord Jesus Christ as my personal Savior.

To be more clear "accepted the Lord" for me was the realization that I knew something was missing (an unexplainable void). I felt fatherless even though my dad was in the house. Accepting the Lord for me meant I had direction; direction greater than myself. A connection with my creator. It felt like I was living in the land of the blind which now I can see.

# DRIVEN BY F.I.R.E.

When I say I accepted the Lord, it doesn't mean that if you accept the Lord you will be a millionaire or that everything will be rosy. Sadly, there are tons of great Christian men and women who are not happy. But for me, the Lord was my starting point.

At twelve years of age, He became my Rock, my Foundation.

As I got older, things became a little more challenging. As a student, I was pretty bad. My grades were decent, but I was more focused on sports, girls, and having fun.

I had the gift of gab, and this became the new issue between my dad and me. Talking landed me in several detentions at school.

My dad did not play around with what he considered foolishness. He did not care if you were twelve or eighteen, he did not play games. If he thought I needed a punishment, I would get one. If he needed to "lay" hands on me he would, and I'm not talking about "laying hands" on you for praying.

He was trying to put me onto a course that he felt was right for me.

I learned to be afraid of my mistakes. And it made my internal compass a bit difficult to follow. I wanted to please my parents, and I also wanted to just be a kid.

But this situation is typical. Heck, I even know some people who still have trouble getting their parents to acknowledge (and love) who their children are.

There's more.

Once upon a time, I had a great fear of public speaking. Sure, I was a talker, but I surely wasn't going to talk in public. In fact, I would avoid it at all costs every time it came up.

Why? I stuttered badly. This behavior made me very uncomfortable and extremely nervous about speaking before people. It was completely humiliating, as well as embarrassing.

But I knew that had to change. I knew I had to change this part of me if I wanted more from my life.

And I wanted more. My dad pushed me in that direction too.

(See? The Lord was navigating all along, even if it didn't feel like it.)

We all know that at twelve **you don't know what you don't know**, but I knew that I was going to leave the house, 'knew' being the operative word.

I did not know how, but I knew it would happen.

I wanted to be away from the situation that I was in.

I wanted to change my stutter.

I wanted more from my life – so much more.

And even though I didn't see anything changing just yet, **I believed** it could.

Sometimes, that's exactly what needs to happen first – to believe. While we all want to have this moment where we can see into our future, and see exactly what's going to happen, if we don't believe in the possibilities before us, that vision is going to be cloudy. There is a great book that I love which says, "Lean not on your own understanding, but acknowledge him in all your ways, and He will direct your path." (Proverbs 3:5 paraphrased)

Instead, we need to start thinking about how we believe in ourselves, really, truly, deeply. God believes in us, so why not try this out in our own lives?

Stop and at least tell yourself that you will TRY to believe in what your future can look like, and what it WILL be like.

When you start believing in yourself, even before you can see things happen, you are setting yourself up for success. Let's look at this from a different viewpoint because I know this can be a bit difficult to digest at first.

What happens when you start feeling confident in yourself? When you believe in yourself and in who you are and what you do, you are a strong and powerful person.

You walk into a room with authority and you talk to people as though you know what you're talking about (because you do).

You are fully present in your life, and you believe that good things will happen – or you believe that when not-so-good things happen, you can handle it.

You BELIEVE in yourself. And things happen. Good things.

It all starts with believing in what you want and in who you are. After all, you're the only one who can do the believing. No one else can believe in you and make you feel that confidence. Maybe for a short time, having the support of a loved one or a family member can boost your confidence, but after a while, you need to take on the job for yourself.

Perhaps you even start with some 'fake it until you make it.' Maybe you need to start believing in the great things that will happen in your life RIGHT NOW. Never forget *"if you can see it in your mind, you can hold it in your hands."*

Just continue to tell yourself that wonderful things are before you, until you believe it.

The best part is that right when you start to believe in it, you will begin to see that your attitude has shifted your life and navigated you to the right road.

You'll get proof that all of that *positive thinking* has led you to where you need to be.

The secret is that you need to believe it before you see it. Only when you have truly, truly taken in something as being true can you begin to see it show up in your life.

# SET YOUR COURSE

When you get into your car, you don't drive around in circles. Well, you might do that once in a while, but eventually, you need to end up somewhere.

You need to end up in a place you want or need to go.

This is where things can get sticky for some people. You might completely understand the concept of believing in yourself and in good things, but how can you choose the good things you want?

How can you set the course to your amazing life?

Yes, you need to make a decision. You need to decide what you want from your life, and you need to figure out where you want to go when all is said and done in your hard work and your efforts.

Where do you want to go?

If your answer is 'not here,' you'll have to be more specific than that. In fact, the more specific you are, the better your chances are of getting that very thing or situation to come into reality.

There are a few things you need to know about me right now. I believe in the power of the mind. I believe in the power of your thoughts and how they can change the direction of your life.

(Anyone who has had a bad day can see how this is true. You think you're going to have a bad day, and you do. If you truly think your day will be good, your day will be good.)

Because I believe this, I want to pass this on to you. Sure, you might not think this is the right way to live your life just yet, but you might shift your perspective once you see how rapidly your life adjusts to suit your thoughts (and not the other way around).

Of course, I also believe that God is there to align my life with my thoughts when they are positive and in accordance with his plan.

If you don't make any decision about where to go, you'll feel and be stuck in your life.

Making the decision to go for what you want is the crux of accomplishing any goal. The 'how' will show up once you have made the decision to make it happen.

When you finally tap into the greatest goal of your life and you find the direction you are called to go, you will figure out the 'how.' I've always found that once I believed in what I was doing, I could see the next steps.

> **"Lean not on your own understanding, but acknowledge Him in all of your ways, and He will direct your path." (Proverbs 3:5, paraphrased)**

Don't worry about the path; it will reveal itself.

I made the decision to get out of the house at an early age, even though I did not know how I would do it. This example from my life reveals the power of decision.

But let's also look at the word 'decision' for a clue about what else we do when we make a choice to head in a certain direction.

If the word incision means 'to cut into' and the word excision means 'to cut out,' you can see why decision means to 'cut off.'

When you make a decision, you cut away and you cut off the other opportunities around you. You commit to one direction and one path for your life (at least for now).

You choose to only focus on one direction and give all of your attention to it. You choose to give all of your energy to that one thing that you decided to call your own.

Imagine what happens when all of your attention and all of your energy is in ONE DIRECTION.

That's where beautiful things emerge and where believing becomes seeing.

But what if you're afraid of cutting away all of the other possibilities in your life?

What if you're the type of person who likes shiny objects and who is always looking for the next best thing to do?

(Confession: I do this too!)

When you allow your focus to be scattered or you choose to not make one decision, you are creating a scattered energy in your life. You are creating confusion about where your direction really is.

Instead, think about razor sharp focus.

Think about dedication instead of not being able to do everything you want.

Remember, when you put your mind to it, you can achieve anything.

And the best news? You're not alone – and you don't have to be the only passenger in the car.


# CHOOSING YOUR PASSENGERS

So, I talked about the importance of being clear. The next arrow in your quiver of success is the power of counsel.

Translation: You need a support team.

I don't care how young or old you are, the power of good counsel is extremely important during your struggle and vital to your success. Everyone has a blind spot or two or ten.

Good advice clarifies questions and produces perspective.

> **"Plans succeed through good counsel; don't go to war without wise advice." ~ Proverbs 20:18**

As my faith grew stronger in myself and in the Lord, I was constantly pondering and praying about my big question, "How am I going to get out of south Florida?"

I knew I was willing to do anything. I knew I was ready to do anything, but I also found myself unsure of the path to take.

I had a few ideas in mind, but some were not as practical as I thought they needed to be.

I continually asked myself, "What is the realistic way to get out of this situation?"

It came to me suddenly – college. More specifically college football. I realized I already had an advantage that others did not. I was an athlete and a pretty good one.

I played football at my high school, and I realized that if I worked harder on developing my skills and building up my statistics, I might be able to get a university to notice me.

And to give me a scholarship.

So I started to get specific about what I wanted. I set my sights on the University of Florida, with the eventual goal to play in the NFL.

It all made complete sense. I was going to go places and my talents on the field were going to be my ticket out of South Florida.

## BAKERS AND BUTLERS

This is a great place to talk about the Bakers and the Butlers.

It sounds like it's off topic, but hang in here for a moment.

Bakers are the ones who have the recipe for your success, while Butlers will open doors to your success.

Bakers are the individuals that bake the cookies and the cakes and the good stuff that we like. But first they gather all of the recipes and the proper ingredients.

Butlers open doors in your life. They help you when you're ready to walk through the door and they show you the way when you can't see it for yourself.

I will mention a couple of Bakers and Butlers I have met in my lifetime because seeing them in action is the best way to recognize these people in your own life.

## LOVED ONES

As cliché as it might sound, my wife at the time had been a rock for me. She was the main Baker and the Butler in my life, bringing me the good things and showing me the way. She had a way to harness my engine like a governor on a Ferrari. She had a strategic focus vs. my full speed focus (get out of the cave, cook it, and eat it mentality). Both are needed but speed without strategy is a train wreck and strategy without playing full speed is delusional if you're going to reach success in any area of life.

And I didn't always appreciate it. Sometimes, I flat out ignored what she had to offer me. I completely disregarded what she had to say and I kept plundering forward as though I knew what to do.

But she had a different perspective, and she could point out what I might have wanted to do instead. She was the voice that sometimes whispered in my ear or yelled in my face.

I need that. You need that. You need some loved ones in your life to be a passenger on this journey. It's not that they are a person who will always tell you how perfect you are; rather you need a person who is going to tell you how it really is.

You need a truthful voice that speaks up when you need a truth, and someone who will be there to hold you when things aren't going the way you expected.

They are the Bakers and the Butlers, and they are there to help you stay on the road (or they might help you see that you're heading in the wrong direction).

## FRIENDS

The friends I've had in my life have come and gone, and I used to be upset by things. But now I realize how some people are meant to be in your life for a short time, to give you instant direction before they head off into another person's world.

The reason why I've separated friends from loved ones is that you also need people who love you, but who are not always in the same room or location as you are.

You need someone who has the outside view of your life and is ready to tell you when things need to change.

There are the people who you ask for help or for support. They might also be the person who you ask to just sit there and listen to you when you need an ear.

Or they can be the person who takes your mind off thin, makes you feel happy again.

Turning to the right friends is essential, however. It's better to talk to friends who are positive and who are there to help you, rather than talking to the friends who simply want to tell you that you're dreaming.

You're not dreaming. You're setting the course for your happiness. Steve Jobs was a "dreamer", Bill Gates was a "dreamer", Oprah Winfrey was a "dreamer"......just saying.


## MY COACH'S COUNSEL

One of my first Butlers was Coach Cannon, my athletic director in high school. He was like a second dad to me. A tough SOB, he didn't listen to excuses.

He taught me lessons I have never forgotten: ***good character, personal responsibility, and hard work.***

Coach Cannon was vigilant about developing character. He used to say: "Who you be speaks so loud that nobody hears what you're saying."

I know the grammar ain't right but here's what he meant directly: Basically, ***don't run your mouth*** just show me your ***consistent actions***.

(This is paraphrased from Ralph Waldo Emerson's quote: "Don't say things. What you are stands over you the while, and thunders so that I cannot hear what you say to the contrary.")

Coach's philosophy was action or character in motion. He watched our actions, not just what we said when we were around him. He taught me that the ***things no one sees you do are the things that everyone wants***.

He said, "Your life is like a canvas, a painting. It may not be a perfect picture, but it's your picture. So when you make a mistake, do not pull out the whiteout, but own up to it, admit it and go on."

**He taught me that mistakes are going to happen**, and though I have failed in the past, I am not a failure. You win some in life, and you learn some (you only lose if you quit).

Notice, I did not say you win some and you lose some, because through failure, if your perspective is right, you learn.

**That's where success begins – in learning from mistakes**.

The next thing Coach Cannon taught me was taking personal responsibility. On the football field, he used to scream, "If every man does his job and takes personal responsibility, we will score!"

In scrimmage one day, he called the "36 – dive" play. We broke the huddle and kind of casually walked up to the line to execute the play. His whistle shrieked.

"Is that how we break the huddle? Do it again!" he shouted.

We huddled again, shouted, "Ready! Break!" We sprinted quickly toward the line.

Just before the ball was hiked, he blew the whistle again and shouted, "Do it again! If you don't run it right this time, everyone on offense is going to run wind sprints the rest of practice. Every man! Take responsibility!"

All of the offense now shook our heads and said, "Oh crap."

(Though I don't think 'crap' was the word we used.)

None of us wanted to run wind sprints in that hot Florida weather. So everyone held themselves and their teammates on offense responsible to get their man. For about fifteen minutes, we ran that same play until we got it right.

Each time the defense stuffed us at the line of scrimmage, Coach Cannon screamed, "Run it again! Every man do your job!"

They stuffed us again, and he said, "Run it again, dang it! 36 – Dive! Let's go!"

We were thinking, *We have run this stupid play over and over, Coach, we know it.*

But Coach understood that repetition is the mother of skill, so repeat it we did - over and over - until we came flying out of the huddle and moved the ball deep into the secondary.

Success! We took personal responsibility to execute and each of us got our man!

> *"Repetition is the mother of skill. Repetition is the seed of learning." ~ Unknown*

Coach had instilled in us what the great Vince Lombardi was famous for saying, "You never win a game unless you beat the guy in front of you. The score on the board doesn't mean a thing. That's for the fans. You've got to **win the war with the man in front of you**. You've got to get your man."

Always take personal responsibility for where you are in your life and never blame people or circumstances.

The last lesson was on hard work. In fairness, my dad was my first real mentor in teaching me to work hard. Though he was not perfect, he showed me what hard work looked like.

I never really understood his work ethic because he never showed me the 'why' behind it. He just did the work.

And with my dad, you did not ask many questions. If you did, you did not get many answers. Coach Cannon showed me how and why to work, while my dad drove me to work.

***The only time "success" comes before "work" is in the dictionary***. Nothing, I mean nothing, replaces hard work! To overcome adversity, struggles, and end up on top, you have to develop the mental attitude of hard work. Winners in life, true winners, we see as in athletes, have this characteristic and so can you.

You must leave the cave, go kill it, bring it back, and cook it before you can eat it.

***You need to learn to love hard work***.

As the Bible says in Proverbs 10:4 from the New Living Translation, "Lazy people are soon poor; hard workers get rich." Getting rich is not just money, you'll find being wealthy in ALL areas of your life is what you're looking to accomplish. Being "Lazy" and being poor as the scripture says has way more to do than with just money.

Coach Cannon was honest too. He explained how the likelihood of playing Division 1 football was a long shot, and how hard it was to make it to the NFL. He said, "If you work hard, harder than you think you can, you've got a shot." But he knew the real lesson is in the process not the outcome. Being honest enough to say "it's a long shot" which it was, but pushing me to keep working towards something was the value.

# LOOK OUT FOR HELP

Look for Bakers and Butlers in your life.

Regardless of your age, the Lord will always send people into your life who have the recipe and the ingredients you need to succeed. And they definitely have what you need to get you through the struggle.

First, you must **open your eyes** wide to notice them, and once you find them, **be willing to listen** to their counsel. God will always put people in your life, but only you can **make the choice** to listen or allow them to speak into your life.

Do you have Bakers and Butlers in your life right now? Are you choosing to listen to them?

Having the right passengers in your vehicle toward success is what matters most in the beginning. Over time, while you'll still need help, you might not need as much help as you do when you're starting out.

I still turn to the people in my life who are willing and able to help me, but I also have a foundation of good information in my mind and in my heart.

Now, I can become the Butler or the Baker for you.

## MANUFACTURER RECOMMENDATIONS

Are you ready to decide? Can you make a decision to cut off all possibilities or excuses that get in the way of moving toward success in your life? If so, list your 'why' for moving forward.

#1 - Decision Time
What are three reasons, circumstances or excuses used in your past that have been barriers to success?

List the top two decisions of change that you have made.

What does 'decide' mean?

The plan is not as important as the decision! The plan will show up, but you must be willing to cut off all limiting possibilities or barriers (Proverbs 3:5-6).

## #2 – Bakers and Butlers

It is important to realize that there is no 'self-made' person in life. I know some of you may disagree, but the fact of the matter is that we all have had some type of counsel (Proverbs 15:22) or people that have led us to new discoveries and success.

This is not to undermine the power of one's will, nor is it for any one person to take credit for your successes or your failures; you own both.

No one can take credit for your work or lack thereof. List five of the Bakers and Butlers in your life that have led you, or have the potential to lead you, to new discoveries.

1. _____

2. _____

3. _____

4. _____

5. _____

## #3 – Your Blind Spot

List two reasons why you have not sought out your Bakers and Butlers. Why have you not listened to them in the past?

1._____
_____

2._____
_____

## #4 – Taking Responsibility

List three circumstances in your life in which you have blamed others for your lack of success.

1. _____

2. _____

3. _____


I will no longer blame anyone, anything or any circumstance in my life for my results. I am personally responsible.

# 3 – WHEN YOUR DASHBOARD LIGHTS COME ON

You've thought about what you want to believe and you've started to assemble the perfect passengers for this journey.

Now what?

You prepare for something to happen. Just as you want to take your car into the shop on a regular schedule to make sure everything is okay, you also want to prepare for things to not quite work out the way you expected.

Remember what we said about things starting to fall in place once you **make a decision?**

Well, what I didn't say is that sometimes, you might not like the way things fall together.

In fact, you might truly believe that something isn't working.

## SOMETHING'S NOT WORKING

*"One's best success comes after his greatest disappointments." ~ Henry Ward Beecher*

We have talked about clarifying what you want, about making a decision and cutting off all other options, and the value of hard work.

But what if you do all those things and still don't succeed?

What if you follow every single concept of this entire book and you don't see your life become instantly amazing?

It's okay.

Even though you may have been brought up to think that failure is the worst thing that could happen to you, think again. Failure is an opportunity.

This is the point in my young life where I was devastated.

Here I was, an eighteen-year-old kid focused on getting out of my dad's house, being my own man, and looking to play college football at the University of Florida.

I pushed myself, worked out, ran wind sprints and paid the physical price, but still got the biggest shock of my life. You see, my faith in myself was huge, and my faith in the Lord was strong, and I just knew I was going to play Division 1A football and eventually go to the NFL.

I was wrong. I didn't know it at the time, but I was dead wrong.

I remember it clearly. February 6, 1992 was signing day for all high school football athletes in the state of Florida. I had taken my SAT college placement test in December and was pretty confident that everything would work out.

I felt good when I took the test. I was the first to finish, as usual. A 700 score on the SAT was all I needed to be eligible to play Division 1A football and to get a scholarship at that time (I think you got 500 just for putting your name on the paper).

True, I was never a scholar, but I had some pretty good grades, and I took AP economics and AP history in high school, so I felt this test would be easy.

In my own mind, the fact that I had finished first assured me that I had done well. When January rolled around, I anxiously checked the mail every day for my results.

I will never forget receiving my test scores. It was a Tuesday. When I got home that day, my mom said, "Louie, you have some mail."

## DRIVEN BY F.I.R.E.

I became really nervous. In fact, I didn't open the envelope up in front of any one because I was so nervous. In my gut, I felt bad news was coming. Why? At that time in my life my belief in myself was low. I had been told numerous times "you won't play college football". As you typically relate to the same sex parent, what my dad thought of me was super important and let's just say he was no Tony Robbins. He was not the type to encourage or motivate me in that way. Always "not good enough" was his way of pushing me.

I was so nervous that I got in my car, drove down the street away from the house. I stopped and parked the car.

Things seemed to slow down, as I prepared to tear the envelope. I pulled out the letter and found out. There it was: 680. Just 20 points short of eligibility.

I lost it. I completely lost it.

My only thought was, *Why, Lord? Why? This environment isn't good for me, and I thought we had a deal.*

I started crying.

*How in the world am I going to play college football now?*

*How am I going to get out of this house?*

I knew if I didn't get a scholarship, my dad would not pay for my college education. He wasn't a big fan of college. His opinion was that I should stay at home and work for the company business (he owned J&K Roofing for many years and been highly successful) and learn how to make money.

He always asked me, "What are you going to do if you go to college?"

In my mind, I was going to play football, but my standard response was, "Oh, I'm going to be a teacher and a coach." All my dad could think about was how much it would cost to get that four-year degree and then make only a teacher's salary afterward.

He knew I could work with the business and make much more money.

When something happens that you don't expect, it can be crushing. I know it and I'm sure you know it too.

You have something planned out in your head, you have the image in your mind about what it's going to feel like to succeed and you can taste victory.

And then you're let down.

It's crushing. You begin to question everything. You begin to question who you are and all the work you put into getting where you are at the moment.

You can't believe it.

You doubt you were on the right path. But is that the right way to think during this situation? Is that in line with thinking positively and having faith that you will be shown the way?

Take a deep breath.

Breathe in and think about the things you have learned up to this point of the process. When something goes awry, there's an opportunity for you to do something about it.

Winners win and Losers lose. It's a mentality that has to be developed if you are gonna be successful in anything in life. Resilience! Like a rubber band, YOU MUST BOUNCE BACK.

For example, I could have learned to give up. I could have learned to sit in a room and feel sorry for myself about not getting to live out my dream.

Instead, I realized I had an opportunity to find another way out of the house. And that is exactly what happened.

# WHERE'S YOUR FUEL TANK?

*"Love is measured by heartbeats. Hope is measured by faith.
Life is measured by living. Happiness is measured by choice."*
~ *Charles Madison*

Sometimes, we don't realize it. We don't realize we're running on empty. We're moving along, but we don't have the energy or the drive to keep going.

But we know we need to keep moving, so we do. We keep moving as though our life depended on it, and we don't get anywhere we want to go.

And we're frustrated.

**It is hard to see the picture when you are stuck inside the frame**. In reflecting upon the stage of my life in which I planned and worked hard to get out of my parents' house, I see that I could not connect the dots of those events until I was past them.

You just don't know what you don't know.

In my home, I was not surrounded with a loving environment, and I give my parents no hall pass for how they dealt with me. However, I am who I am because of my parents. My point of sharing this chapter is 100% directed to any of you who are reading this book and may be making excuses, whining or complaining about your environment. Why would I direct this toward you? Because you can choose who you want to be, **regardless of your circumstances.**

I've been exposed to drugs, violence, alcohol, emotional drama, physical drama and gambling growing up in South Florida. However, being exposed to this environment doesn't mean that I get to make any excuses or do those things. Your environment has no power over you if you choose to change it to the positive.

I'm reminded of the old story of the two boys who grew up with an abusive, alcoholic father. He was the town drunk who was never a good example or role model for his family. One son grew up to be a successful CEO of a major corporation, while the other grew up to be a drunk.

When, as adults, they were interviewed about their upbringing, they were asked why their lives had turned out as they had.

They both replied, "With a dad like mine, how could I turn out to be anything else?" The moral is you can make the decision to be successful, regardless of your past or current environment.

Because success is very subjective, it is time for you to start changing your mindset to achieve your own personal triumphs. Think about what you're hungry for? What fills up your internal fuel tank and keeps you going – no matter what? **What excites you so much it keeps you up at night?**

For many, it could be to make a lot of money or to have a bigger home.

Think long and hard about what you really want and what is driving you forward. It doesn't have to be something that is pretty or simple or even something you share with others.

But you need to have something in your fuel tank, something to keep you going when things get tough and you're wandering around without any idea of the direction you need to take.

I had to develop an appetite for success. "It's good for workers to have an appetite, an empty stomach drives them on" (Proverbs 16:26). I had to get hungry. It started at about eighteen years of age when I heard someone say, "Food is for the hungry, not for the needy."

What is your why? For me, (at that time) it was all about not returning home to my dad and having him tell me he was right.

There's a bigger picture here too, one that you might not be able to see or one that you may not want to see when you're running low on fuel and passion.

I had to, by faith, understand that going to the University of Florida was not part of the plan. (As destiny would have it, I was going to play football, but in Lynchburg, Virginia.)

**God has a purpose for your pain, a reason for your struggle, and most importantly, a reward for your faithfulness.**

In the meantime, it is your responsibility to develop an appetite for success.


# FILLING UP ON FAITH

> *"Fear knocked on the door, faith opened it, and there was no one there." ~ Unknown*

The "f" word is the strongest word in the dictionary. Even if you don't use it, even if you don't like it, you can't discount its power.

But when I say the "f" word, I'm not referring to what most people think of when they hear it.

I'm talking about faith or fear.

The big question is, which "f" word dominates you? Faith or fear?

It's interesting to note that these two words are obviously different, yet they are reciprocal spiritual forces.

Hebrews 11:1 says, "Now **faith** is the substance of **things hoped for**." Fear is just the opposite. Fear is the substance of things not hoped for or desired – of course, I don't need to tell you that.

We all avoid fear and things that frighten us. We move in the opposite direction of the things that scare us – because they aren't always predictable. We don't know what might happen.

And often, we assume that the unknown is filled with bad things.

As Job 3:25 says, "That which I have so greatly feared has come upon me."

What you need to remember too is that while fear is scary and can lead us down darker paths, it's also a motivator. When we're afraid, we can also choose to face those fears.

Just like Job did.

That said, you have to have **faith** in yourself to know that you can **face your fears head on.** You need to be sure of yourself and your part in the world.

You need to have faith in God to know that no matter what fears rest in your heart, you can still persevere because you're being watched out for – you're in good hands.

However, when you let fear take over, when you let your reserves of faith get too low, you're going to hesitate. You're going to be waiting around for your life to be easy and safe and expected. That means you will be waiting a long time. If you look at a week—there are Tuesdays, and Fridays, BUT there is never a SOMEDAY. Play to win, not play to lose.

It doesn't work like that. What does work is realizing there is a relationship between faith and fear – and you're the one that can make the most of this information.

## MY STORY CONTINUES

As I looked for how I could leave my home, I talked with my high school coach about my available options.

35

He told me, "We had very little interest from many schools since your SAT scores were so low and your level of competition was sub par."

It was true. I had played in a Division 1A high school, the lowest level of competition in high school sports. Though football was pretty good at all levels in south Florida, our small private Christian school played against some major talents (Danny Kanell went on to become a Florida State Seminole football star and played for the New York Giants and the Atlanta Falcons; I played against A-Rod even), but still I wasn't getting noticed.

My coach had been involved with Liberty University back in the days of Eric Green who had gone on to play tight end for the Pittsburgh Steelers and the Miami Dolphins. Because of that, he told me he would call Liberty and see what they could do for me.

Part of my whole dream of playing professional football was still an option because of Coach Sam "Riverboat" Rutigliano, then a coach at Liberty. He coached the Cleveland Browns back in the late seventies and early eighties when they were called the Cardiac Kids. I figured if I could play around a coach that recognized NFL talent, maybe I was still in the game if I proved myself.

But I'll never forget the day when my coach broke the news to me that Liberty University wasn't going to offer me a full scholarship, but I could walk on and possibly get some assistance with books.

Talk about having your faith tested. I truly thought I had a chance to play Division 1 football, but I couldn't even get a scholarship for Division1AA. Truth be told, there actually had been some offers made from Division 2, but my ego was too big. So I was heading to Lynchburg, despite my lack of enthusiasm, and low spirit.

Strangely enough, this experience opened my eyes. I was wrong about my Dad. He knew I wanted to play football, so he paid for that first year of school at Liberty. Books and food were provided by the school. I thought I would be 100% on my own financially, so this came as quite a surprise, even a shock. He paid for my private schooling (high school) and then my first year of college.

Like so many other people, my mom wasn't happy I was leaving, as she'd just as soon have me around forever. And I couldn't wait to leave.

Every time I tried to communicate with my mother from college, which wasn't very often, it would create problems. My dad did not want her to be in contact with me (or so I thought).

One critical day in my life, a conversation with my mom became a dividing point in our relationship. I explained to her that every time we tried to communicate there was always a serious issue with Dad.

"We are probably better off just not communicating," I told her.

Maybe I was looking for an excuse or reason to stop talking to her and to my dad. To this day, I'm not exactly sure what was happening, or what happened in that moment. I just knew I was frustrated and ready to step away and onto my own path.

A path that didn't include the drama.

Faith or fear – the choice stared me in the face.

"This is it. I am finally on my own," I said to myself after I hung up the phone.

It was kind of like driving in your car and seeing the rearview mirror. You can't move forward if you spend time looking back. I wasn't going to spend any more time looking back.

During my drive up the Blue Ridge Mountains, I started to tear up, realizing that it was just the Lord and me. That was the moment where my relationship with the Lord grew strong and my faith fully developed.

At that moment, I began to cry. I was on my own, an eighteen-year-old without anyone else in the world but myself. And I was trying to hold it together.

But in that moment, I had to just break apart. Anyone would. It was terrifying and it was new and it was scary. I didn't know what might happen next. The thought of my son or daughter having a conversation like that with me at eighteen years old now is mind blowing. I was confused, crushed, and scared. How would I get money? Do I need to get a job? Then of course that inner voice (fear) screamed at me, "be careful what you wish for Louie".

As I drove, however, my faith overtook my fear. I remembered the verse in Romans 8:28, "All things work together for the good of those who love Him and are called according to His purpose."

Somehow, despite all reason and all understanding, I had a feeling deep in my belly that everything was going to be all right.

I stopped worrying about the 'how.' I stopped looking for reasons to not do what I wanted to do.

*I just went forward, in faith.*

In truth, I was never alone – and you are never alone. As in Hebrews 13:5, the Lord said, ***"I will never leave you nor forsake you."*** I always knew that I had faith, and I had confidence in that faith. It enabled me to not have to walk in fear.

Fear knocked on the door, faith opened it, and there was no one there.


## PLAYING THE GAME

During the first year of playing for Liberty University, the coaches wanted to move me to defense. But I just knew I was a tight end. After all, I was 6'3" and 258 pounds.

And the truth of the matter is that Dwayne Carswell who was one year ahead of me was my direct competition. He was a good guy, great football player and unfortunately for me, just a better player. He went on to play for the Denver Broncos for fifteen seasons, and I would have to make some decisions.

I knew I could play tight end at this level but I had to ask myself the question. Would I play defense, or would I leave the team?

I called my old high school coach, and I said, "I want to play right away, and it doesn't look like I'm going to play. I want to transfer to another school, so what are my options?"

Before I go on, I know how rash this sounds. It sounds like I gave up before I even tried to do something different. And it sounds like I was someone who wanted everyone else to take care of me. I get that's the way this comes across, but stick with me for a moment.

Let's remember that this is also a story about faith in one's self.

As we chatted on the phone, he said, "Send me some scrimmage film. We will put it all together, look at it, and I'll see what is available."

Now, fortunately for me, Coach Cannon had worked in Georgia prior to coming to Florida, so he knew some people there.

He called me back to say, "I have a school available, and they are willing to give you some scholarship money. They are also willing to help you get some programs set up that will take care of the balance of your out-of-state tuition. Technically, though, you still have to walk on the football team."

Instead of being grateful, I have to admit my first response was, "Good Lord, here we go again. Why is this happening to me all over again?"

Instead of saying, "Why me?" I should have said, "Try me."

Yes, it was a struggle. Yes, I had to pack up my things (again) and move, but it ended up being the pivotal moment in my life.

But as I processed through this frustration and disappointment, I said to myself, "I just want to play."

I asked the coach, "Where's the school?"

"West Georgia College in Carrollton, Georgia."

And I said to myself, "Where in the world is Carrollton?" he explained it was near Alabama, almost on the Alabama-Georgia line.

*God, I don't know anybody in Georgia, but I'll do it,* I thought to myself.

I packed all my stuff, got all of my transcripts transferred, and organized my paperwork. Before I knew it, I was headed to Carrollton from Lynchburg, Virginia, not knowing a soul or who would be there when I got there.

This journey was different than the last time.

During the drive from Lynchburg to Georgia, instead of being frustrated, I became fascinated. My faith was growing. The reality was the Lord was with me, and I didn't cry this time. I knew the Lord was watching out for me, and that I was going to be pleasantly surprised.

The shift from **frustration to fascination** gives you the opportunity for appreciation instead of aggravation, turning the negative tone of the situation into anticipation.

But how do you move from fear into faith?

How do you feed your faith instead of your fear?

It's easy enough for me to tell you that you *should*, but it's another thing for you to know what that means.

What I will tell you is that you don't have to get on a football team and then ask to be assigned to a new team in order to get what you want. I know your life looks different from mine.

So, let's talk about how you can start thinking about feeding your faith.

> **Practice your faith** – If you're not already praying on a regular basis, I highly recommend it. You should be focusing on how you can connect with God and how you can interact with Him on a regular basis. Just like any relationship, it helps if you talk regularly. Pray about your fears, pray for faith. You will get what you need when you reach out.

> **Count your blessings** – So often, fear emerges when we stop thinking about what is right with our lives. Instead of thinking only about what is wrong, stop and count all of the blessings you have. Stop and think about what went RIGHT today, as opposed to what went wrong. There's always something to be grateful about. Gratitude leads to more in life.

> **Look for the bright side** – This is similar to the previous piece of advice, but it's invaluable. Always try to find something positive about the things that are happening in your life. When you dwell on the negative or you try to find things that are wrong, you will most likely find that something is wrong. Since life isn't perfect, that's guaranteed. Instead of using your energy on negative thoughts, try directing your energy to finding what's great about your life.

You can also feed your faith by giving thanks during times when your faith is tested.

Let's be clear, while I'd love to think you're going to read this book and instantly be able to have all the faith you need, it's not the most realistic situation.

I still have times when I think things are not working out the way I want them to. I still have days when I ask why things are happening in a way I don't want them to happen.

But the stronger my faith has become, the less time I spend in the negative and fearful thinking.

And you can spend less time on fear when you start feeding the faith you have. You already have the faith. Now, appreciate it and use it.

Feed your faith and not your fears. When you are attacked by doubts, doubt your doubts, not your faith! Don't get caught up in the 'what if's.'

**Scenario sickness** is a bad disease. Don't get caught up in this sickness for the only medication for it is Faith and Belief in where you are going.

Live your life in the amazement of knowing that you are being watched over by God – and He's not going to let you down.


# MOVE FORWARD...OR NOT?

*"You are always committed to something, and what you are committed to shows up most often." ~ Mike Jones*

With all of this talk about fear and faith, it becomes clear that there are times when you won't know what to do.

And sometimes, there may very well be situations when your fear is accurate or your faith is wobbly.

In those times, there may be the question about whether you should move forward in your life or not. I can't really answer that question for you, though I can tell you that I've had the most success when I listened to my gut and went for what I thought was right.

But I want you to ask another question of yourself: are you committed to or just interested in living out your dream in life?

How you answer this important question is a major factor in whether you will design a life of **significance** or just make a living of **survival.**

Being committed or just interested are two separate worlds. People who are just interested often find themselves living in survival mode. These people are not focused on being great but on doing enough to get by.

These are the people in your life who might frustrate you because you know they can have more and be more. (Or you might not notice them at all because they don't stand out.)

People often start a new adventure with the thought of being committed, only to realize later that they were just 'interested.'

(Think about how many people start the New Year with the intention of getting in shape, but come February they are less than enthused about their ideas and their commitment. After all, there's always next year...)

Having a full-fledged commitment to something, whether it's a marriage, a job, or even a college degree, takes every bit of your being.

The way I've learned it is everything in life takes ten times the effort, ten times the work, ten times the attitude, and ten times the emotion you projected before you started.
Author and sales trainer Grant Cardone calls this the 10X rule. The 10X rule is all about your level of commitment. If you're not willing to extend your commitment beyond your initial interest, you may want to rethink your plans. If you really look at the 10X philosophy it's about multiplication not addition or subtraction. 10X is really 100! In short everything worth pursuing is 100X harder than we think.

# DRIVEN BY F.I.R.E.

Are you committed to exercising 10X the energy and effort you thought it would take to achieve your dream? It's okay if you're not. It's always better to be honest with yourself than to simply lie about what you want.

Maybe you want something different.

I know for myself that when I stop and really ask myself that question about whether I am committed, I can determine whether I need to adjust my goals.

You might uncover new goals – ones that you can COMMIT to, not just promise you'll think about or try.

Commitment means a willingness to be in **discomfort**, or even **pain**. But pain is always temporary, and you must be willing to turn pain into prosperity.

Jesus on the cross clearly illustrated this by being willing to suffer, being willing to bear pain, and even being willing to die for the people of the whole world. Thankfully, you don't need to go that far, I imagine, but you need to think about it this way. I promise regardless of your thoughts on Jesus, He was **committed** not **interested**.

What are you willing to do? What actions are you willing to take?

Things aren't always going to be simple. A marriage is the easiest place to find this out. Those honeymoon days are great, but they are not the same days as when you are trying to manage a full-time job and three kids and your wife is sick and you lost your retirement funds in the bad economy.

That is the time when you find out if you are committed.

Let's say you want to start a business. The first thing to do is create a plan. Then you begin to project what you think will happen during the time your business is in business, followed by redoing your projections to be a little more conservative or 'to play it safe.'

Next, you acquire the resources, hire your team and train them. It's a green light, right? Well, maybe. If you are like most people, as soon as it gets tough and circumstances not in your favor start to develop, it will be obvious whether you are committed or just interested.

Some will just give up. Some will just stop what they're doing.

Others will use this moment to find out what they could do better and how they could do MORE.

Negative circumstances will crop up sooner or later. That's life.

Motivational speaker and American business statesman, the late Jim Rohn said, "All good will be attacked." To me, this simply means that no matter if you are positive or negative in life, junk happens.

When it starts to happen, if you have not or choose not to develop mental toughness, pretty soon you become only interested, not committed.

When you lack total commitment, and you start figuring out your Plan B before you even try to make your Plan A work, you're probably not doing what you want to do.

Actor Will Smith has said, "There's no reason to have a Plan B because it distracts you from Plan A."

Think about this for a minute.

We've all been taught that having a Plan B is a good thing. After all, it means we're prepared. **But it also gives us an 'out.'** It allows us to have something there in case we fail.

This assumes there is even a possibility that our Plan A will fail. Instead, we can take our actions on faith and we can move forward with Plan A as far as it will take us.

We can move forward until Plan A simply doesn't work – no matter what we have tried. But we need to try. We need to keep moving, even when everything around us is telling us that we are nuts for believing in whatever we believe in at that moment.

That said, you can still plan...for your success.

# PLAN YOUR TRIP

How committed are you? Can you feel it in your bones and in your heart?

Though it might seem contradictory, your commitment level depends on your map. By map, I don't mean an application on your phone, your GPS system, or even an atlas.

Your map is your mind, and your mental attitude. This is the part of you that has been crafted and honed over years of being in the world. The things you have experienced shape this part of you and the ideas you have been exposed to in your life shape you as well.

Your upbringing, your parents, and your friends have shaped your attitude. And it's not just others around you who have been shaping your brain; your brain has been shaping itself too.

Each time you have a thought, your brain has changed. If you have a thought more than once and more than a few times, your brain creates a path to that thought or conclusion again.

***The more times you think something, the more times you will return to that thought – good or bad***. This isn't just based on my experience; science has found it in the brain too. We create maps to the certain feeling we are used to having. Notice, I didn't talk about how we create maps to feelings we want to have – that's something you need to work on.

In the science of NLP (Neuro-Linguistic Programming), the brain is a series of maps, a series of information about how the world works for an individual person – based on their beliefs about the world.

Just as a map of Yellowstone Park is not the park itself, but a two-dimensional simplification on a piece of paper that has enough information to enable a visitor to navigate through the park, likewise, we humans create maps that may not be indicative of how things really are.

We have our own judgments, ideas, and experiences – and **they're not always based in reality.**

They're based in OUR reality. (But possibly not a subjective reality, the one where emotions don't get involved and where we don't make mistakes because we're human.)

A pilot has various 'maps' related to flying a plane, such as knowledge about engineering, aviation, and weather patterns. These maps allow the pilot to fly a plane and make the right judgment when facing a wide variety of situations in the air.

In the same way, spouses have maps regarding marriage, singers have maps regarding music, and so on. Our maps — a mixture of a measuring gauge and a compass — enable us to make sense of a situation and, therefore, are at the very core of our success in life. Your commitment in life will always be drawn from your map, or life experiences, good or bad.

So what?

So, these maps are something we need to consider and something that we can adjust as we move forward.

The more we know, the more we can apply to our lives, shifting our direction, our attitude and our course.

Perhaps this tool will help.

## THE SEED PRINCIPLE

Picture a **seed**, which represents an **idea**. The idea is supposed to grow up through the ground and become a living, fruit-bearing tree. The only difference between an idea and a belief is the quality of **references** that are **attached to the seed**.

A reference is a supporting belief or concept. In this example, we will call them roots.

Sometimes a person gets an idea about him/herself or something else and plants that seed in the garden of their unconscious mind. Then, once the seed is planted, they go out to collect references (proof). As they get more references, whether positive or negative, they start to give root to the idea.

Once this seed, or belief, gets rooted, it begins to sprout upward and toward the top. The result is a positive - fruit, or a negative - no growth. But remember, it all started out with an idea that someone was **committed** to or perhaps just **interested** in.

I left Virginia and went to Georgia because I was committed to play football, or at least I thought I was. I thought I was committed to go all the way to the NFL.

I believed I was committed to getting a teaching degree. I thought I was committed to showing my family I could make it on my own without them.

And it is there that I got some real life lessons and more struggles, adversities and failures, this time on a higher level.
I arrived on campus with Christian institution credits, so not all of these credits transferred to West Georgia College. That meant that I started out as barely more than a freshman. I had to start over, for the most part.

To be honest, I missed more school than I attended. Needless to say, I was showing my commitment, or should I say, my lack of it.

In order to play football, I did go to class at least two and a half years and barely passed, but I was clearly not 100% committed. I played two years at West Georgia and had fun, but I was nowhere close to being an NFL football player.

And this was just the beginning of what I was about to learn at this school and in my life.

At the moment, I didn't realize I was as uncommitted as I actually was.

At that time, I didn't realize I was being set up for something much more important – hard work.

# WHEN THE SAME PROBLEMS POP UP

My whole life up to this point had been the same similar cycle. The pattern was to have a good attitude, believe things will work out, trust the Lord and then experience another setback.

Sound familiar to you?

Do you feel you are a good person who works hard, yet somehow you end up never getting a break in life?

Let me explain this situation and where it begins. Your philosophy, attitude, and activities, or what I call disciplines, equal your results.

If you make the commitment to your dream (goals), your struggles and setbacks work for you, not against you. Catch this – Your setbacks are GIFTS. You need to accept that now, because there are two certainties in life. You will get more setbacks and taxes of course.

When I was younger, I thought that if you prayed about things, you were a good person. God would give you what you wanted, no questions asked and no effort needed.

# DRIVEN BY F.I.R.E.

Glad I figured that one out.

Remember, David defeated Goliath, but not on his knees. Noah didn't build the ark from the sofa while he was watching the latest reality show. They had to move, take positive action, and so do you.

Prayer is good and positive thinking is good. And yes, God grows food for birds, but He's not going to drop it in their nests. The saying goes, "Good things happen to those who wait."

I'm here to tell you, I feel good things happen to those who work their 'blessed assurances' and pay the price for it. My saying goes, "Good things come to those who hustle, and what is left over goes to those who wait."

Of course, this isn't to say you need to hurt yourself in the process or that you shouldn't ever be patient. It is a virtue, after all. But what I mean is that it's better if you don't expect others to take care of you and to help you with your life.

You should be thinking about how you can move those mountains in your way and about how you can show that you're **committed**.

The point is this, I was lazy, lacking focus and totally misdirected. I assumed I would just get everything that I wanted, but I wasn't completely being honest with myself.

And the truth hurts sometimes, but the truth will deliver you. I think this should give us a point to ponder. Are you being honest with yourself? Take a look at your career. Take a look at your relationships. As a spouse, or maybe as a parent, are you being forthright with yourself even now?

Are the same things happening to you? Again and again? Are you feeling frustrated by everything around you?

And are you looking at yourself to see if you're doing all you can? Or are you blaming others and circumstance? If something happens to you once you're a victim. If the same thing happens again and again you now are a volunteer! Don't sign up to be a volunteer.

Honest appraisal and evaluation of your situation and of yourself is going to put you back on the right path to the right destination for your life. What do you have that needs changing? Everybody wants to change others, but ***changing yourself is a full-time job***.

I had all kind of excuses and stories about why I didn't make it to the NFL and all this other stuff, but the reality is that the issue was always me. The issue always starts with me, and it always starts with you. We like to blame others for everything we are going through, but that is not taking personal responsibility.

Because I was a big boy now, all by myself, it was time to continue to figure out how to take care of myself.

I knew I was barely making things work financially, so I decided to work two jobs. I worked at Lowe's (a distribution plant) in Villa Rica, Georgia, loading trucks on a shipping/receiving dock on the graveyard shift. Hated it! Friday- Sunday 6pm-6am. Thirty six hours in three days while my buddies were having fun on the weekends. It sucked! But I had to do it.

I was twenty years old, living with my very good friend Kameron, who was the best man at my wedding. We both worked at Lowe's, but he really hated it. He hated the hours, and he hated the labor. He hated obviously more than me.

So he left and moved on. He decided that Plan B was a better plan for him.

Every weekend, Kameron would get to party since he was working at a restaurant, and I was going to Lowe's on Fridays, Saturdays, and Sundays, sleeping all day, and getting up and doing it again.

## DRIVEN BY F.I.R.E.

This was the most horrible experience of my life. Have you ever been in a job you didn't want to be in, but you needed to in order to get what you wanted?

Again and again, I would come into the same job, get the stickers I needed to put out and do the same thing over and over.

I thought about quitting and going back to Florida. I didn't like what I was doing. I didn't like who I was. I didn't like any of it. But I stuck with it.

Since hindsight is 20/20, I now know that I made the right decision, and that if I'd given up, I would have lost out on something even better.

Have you ever tired out and turned around in the midst of a challenging climb up the proverbial mountain, only to later realize that you were just five feet from the top?

You were almost there, but didn't even know it.

That's where I was at the time. I didn't know I was eight months away from making $75,000 a year, rather than $24,000 at the age of twenty.

"Tough times never last, but tough people do," said Dr. Robert Schuller. And because I was tough, I outlasted the hard stuff.

During this time, I read Napoleon Hill's "Think and Grow Rich." Who knew that such a small book could have such a large impact? It's a must read.

Since then, I have read this book cover to cover at least five times and I recommend it to everybody (including you!). While I didn't read many books in college, I did read this one!

Kameron would always make fun of me and my 'goal board' I had hanging in my room, but it worked and Napoleon Hill was the inspiration.

I wasn't going to get stuck in the same patterns anymore. I wasn't going to settle for being anything less than my best.


# **FALLING FORWARD ON PURPOSE**

Remember that one game you used to play in school or that you may have had to use during a team-building exercise at work, the one that talked about trusting someone else to catch you?

For those who don't know what I'm talking about, it looks like this:

You partner up with someone, or you're in a group of people, and one designated person is tasked with falling backward into the group or into the partner.

They are not supposed to try to stop themselves from falling, nor are they supposed to try to bend their knees or give any sort of hesitation when they move backward.

They're supposed to trust.

But what happens? Most of us don't think others are going to catch us, so we slow down or we bend our knees.

Or we do something else that makes us feel safer about falling. (Which sounds suspiciously like having a Plan B, doesn't it?)

Instead of doing things that prevent failure, I advocate for moving forward and falling forward, even if you're not sure what's going to happen.

This is slightly different from the trust exercise in the example, as it's something you choose to do – and it's something with a purpose. You make the choice to move forward, even if you fall.

This is because you're working on trying to continue to move, even when you're not sure you're going in the right direction.

Or any direction.

You just want to keep moving because that's the way you take action and you stay in the flow of things. You're not just waiting around for things to happen and you're not just waiting around for the perfect situation to arise. Honestly there is never a "perfect" time. There will always be situations that fear disguises as "caution" signs, but have the faith and always move forward.

You're working on the forward motion. You're working on the motion to the end result – even if you don't know what it looks like or what it's going to bring for you.

Here's where the car metaphor starts to break down a bit. When you're trying to figure out what's wrong, you're not going to keep driving, are you?

But you are going to keep going to people who know what might be wrong. You are going to keep looking at different systems to see what might be wrong.

In the end, you may have to keep fixing things until the car seems better. And that still may not work.

However, not trying isn't a solution either. It's a recipe for being stalled forever.

## MANUFACTURER RECOMMENDATIONS

#1 – You Win Some, and You Learn Some
Success in all areas of your life is a journey. Failing is a HUGE part of success. You have to be willing to fail, and you have to recognize that failure is a teacher.

Remember every disappointment is for your development, every event is an education, every test becomes your testimony to live out and show yourself and others that failing is good, not bad. Again, you win some and you learn some.

I was fired four times, and every time something better came along. My mind-sight vs. my eyesight was the difference.

You must work to develop your mind-sight and never get discouraged with setbacks.

List three times in your life where you failed, even though you worked hard. Today, can you see where you grew or got better because of it?


1. _____

2. _____

3. _____

#2 – Change Your Mind
Failure is never final. What can you do to change your mind-sight about failing?

List two new outlooks about failure or failing which you will now adopt as your new mind-sight going forward (notice I did not say "mindset;" mind-sight is something you were able to see/experience, you were able to breathe, you were able to visualize).

1. _____

2. _____

In life you must remember that a setback is usually a setup for something bigger and better. Are you willing to commit to be grateful for every setback?

Make that commitment to yourself now:

I _____ commit to being grateful for the setbacks.

Signed:

Date:

#3 – Clear Your Mind
To develop an appetite for success, you must start the process. You must clean your mind of the clutter you have acquired and renew it. Create the new mindset by reading or listening to podcasts that inspire you.

List three books or podcasts to which you will listen, helping you to change your mindset and spark a new appetite to succeed.

1. _____

2. _____

3. _____

What environment are you in right now that you have to over-come? What do you appreciate about your environment?

_____
_____
_____
_____
_____
_____

## #4 – Changes to Make

List three things you can do now to change your environment, remove yourself from your environment, or have a new mind-set about it and move through it.

1._____
_____

2._____
_____

3._____
_____

Remember, it's hard to see the picture when you're stuck inside the frame. Sometimes it's good to accept that you don't know what you don't know. It's hard to connect the dots until you look back.

Only with experience can people make gains in what they do know.

## #5 – Feeding Your Faith

What can you do to feed your faith? List three different things you can do today.

1. _____

2. _____

3. _____


#6 – Finding Your Frustration
What are you frustrated about? We all know it's not what happens; it's how we respond to what happens that makes the difference for us.

List two items or situations of frustration, so you can learn to be fascinated instead.


1._____

2._____


#7 – Mapping Your Commitment
Have you been committed or interested in your goals and dreams? What has kept you from running all-out towards your commitment?

Your map (beliefs) is not your whole territory. What can you do to increase your level of belief?

List two things you can do to raise your commitment level.


1._____

2._____

#8 – When Problems Happen
A huge part of being successful in any area of life is going from tolerance of adversity to actual appreciation for adversity. Learn to love the challenge; life is filled with hardships! If you

don't learn to value the process of refinement, it will be painful and lead to a lack of success.

List three things you can do to strengthen yourself.

1. _____

2. _____

3. _____

## #9 – Failure Happens, Ending Your Process Doesn't

When you have failed in the past, have you felt like a failure? Failing forward is a huge opportunity for you to grow.

List two times in your life where you failed, but looking back, you learned from it.

Also list what you learned.

1. _____

2. _____

I have learned:

_____
_____
_____
_____
_____
_____
_____
_____
_____
_____
_____
_____

## DRIVEN BY F.I.R.E.

Having a positive mental attitude is huge in overcoming adversity and trials.

List three things you can do today to start building a positive mental attitude:

1. _____

2. _____

3. _____

# 4 - DRIVING IN THE RIGHT LANE

*"With all of your getting, get understanding." ~ Proverbs 4:5*

Just because you know where to go, doesn't mean you know the way to take. More times than not, I ended up in the wrong lane at the wrong time.

Had I realized how I could switch lanes or when I needed to switch lanes, I might have gotten to my destination a bit faster.

Or at least, I would have come to my final destination, where I belonged, much more quickly.

(And with fewer speed bumps.)

## <u>I'LL NEVER GO INTO THE CAR BUSI-NESS!</u>

One of the major keys to life is having **understanding**. It sounds easy initially, but when your life takes turns to the left and right and everything seems upside-down, having a clear understanding is not the easiest thing to do.

In fact, it seems impossible, out of reach, and a pipe dream.

When I dropped out of college and was working at the Lowe's distribution plant in Villa Rica making ends meet, I had no idea that I would also work at Chili's, let alone be in the automotive industry.

Contemplating my situation, I thought to myself, *I can't believe I dropped out of school. I'm officially a college dropout.* I'm not bragging about dropping out, but illustrating my disbelief and **understanding** that things just happen.

Since that time I have learned it's not so much that you get fired, or you drop out, or you leave a relationship as much as it is God at work, moving you from that job or relationship or college. However, when you're right in the middle of everything, you can't see what's happening around you.

And you're definitely not able to understand it all.

As it relates to adversity and struggles, **understanding** is critical to moving forward. When you understand the reason or the direction or even the possibility of what happens next, you can *let go* of your control of what is happening right now. You begin to see that every ending is actually a new beginning.

People search for happiness, but happiness is not a location and it's not a paycheck. It is not a relationship or a car.

Happiness is from within you. You can have all the money in the world, but still be frustrated with your place in life.

It happens time and time again, not because people want it to happen to them, but they may very well have seen it happen.

How many people have seen their parents work to the bone and get all the things they wanted...only to then be unhappy with their lives? Or how many of us pay off our bills and get the big house and still wonder what ELSE we can get?

It's a cycle that you need to stop – if you want your life to be more and attain real success.

Especially if you want to set your life on fire.


**HOW I ENDED UP IN THE LAST PLACE I THOUGHT I'D BE**

One day, my friend Kameron convinced me to come and work with him at a local restaurant. He explained that he was seeing a lot of girls, having a lot of fun, and making much more money than he was making at the distribution plant where we worked together. So I said I would give it a try.

He was right. I loved my new job at Chili's. I had fun and I did meet plenty of girls. But with both jobs combined, I was only making about $2,300 a month.

It wasn't a great situation. But I stuck with it, thankfully.

I'll never forget, a guy from Miami would come in and ask for me every time he ate at the restaurant. Once he knew I was from Miami we had a connection and I thought he was cool. We had fun talking, and I came to know that he was a finance director at the local Honda dealership.

For three months he talked incessantly about getting into the car business. I kept telling him that there was **no way** I would ever sell cars for a living.

Every time I turned him down, he would explain to me how much money the sales representatives made.

He would ask me, "How much money are you making?" I paused every time. I knew that he knew I didn't make what those sales representatives were making.

Not even close.

He would chuckle and say that their sales reps were making twice that much.

After a while, I started to wonder, *What if I made twice as much money as I was making right now? $4,000 to $5,000 a month would make me rich (financially).* And rich sounded better than working two jobs.

I finally struck up the courage to make the decision and give it a shot.

It wasn't simple.

I first made a deal with the Lord. I was sort of like Gideon in the Bible. Even after God had called him, he **asked God for a sign** to prove that He was actually leading him. Have you ever done that?

That night, before going to bed, I asked God, "Lord, would you show me a sign? Any sign? Let me know if this is the direction you want me to go with my life."

Well, that night, like every night, my alarm was set in buzz mode. However, the next morning, the radio on my alarm clock (not buzz) woke me with a car dealership commercial. I sprang out of bed in amazement and confusion.

With that sign, I was convinced selling cars was what I should be doing, even though I was terrified to make this my living.

Even then, I planned for the worst (even with the clear sign). I figured the worst thing that could happen was that I would lose three months of wages if I quit my other two jobs.

I called up the finance director to see what I needed to do for an interview. He told me to wear a shirt and a tie, and to be there by 10:00 a.m.

As I drove to the interview, I talked to myself.

"Man what if I get the job?" I didn't know anything about the car business.

As I walked into the showroom, I expected to be interviewed by a manager. However, I found out that the dealership was small, only selling about 100 cars a month. As a result, the personnel roster was very lean, so I met with the general manager, the top person at the dealership level.

I was a little intimidated, to say the least.

I walked into the room and he asked me why I would be good in the car business. Since I wasn't even looking for a car job,

I had no idea why I would be good in the car business, but that's not what I said.

I took a breath and started **selling** myself. I talked up my strengths and my attitude. I brought in my determination and I looked him straight in the eye as I answered as though I was preparing for this moment my entire life.

(Of course, now, I know that everything I said was absolutely true, even though I hadn't realized it yet.)

Even though I might have thought I was getting interrogated, I came back with an answer to every question he asked. He seemed impressed and I gained more momentum as the conversation continued.

Things went great right up until the very end, when he said, "Son, I think you'd be good, but since this is a small store, we typically don't hire 'onesie-twosie' sales reps. We typically hire several at a time so you can actually get some quality training." In the car industry if you have no experience it's very rare to be hired without any training. Most dealerships won't sit in a conference room for three hours a day to train just one employee.

*Why would he ask me to come up here and interview me if I wasn't going to get the job? Here we go again.* I found my brain heading right back into negative land after hearing that.

I had gone from 'never getting in the car business' to being excited about making $5,000 a month. I had faith and showed up, and now he was telling me I couldn't get the job.

I can say this now, though it wasn't clear at the time. My life would not be the same had I walked out of that office at that moment, because I know for a fact I would never have gotten into the car business, or attempted to, had he let me leave.

So, in that moment, in the spirit of selling, I asked one question that changed my life. As we got up to shake hands, I noticed a Jacksonville State football helmet on the back credenza.

I asked, "Did you play football at Jacksonville State?"

He said, "I did. How did you recognize a helmet from JS?"

I explained how I had gone to Liberty University a couple of years back and played against Jacksonville State in Alabama. Twenty minutes later, after some football talk, he shifted his position.

"Louie, you seem like a good kid. Come to work tomorrow with a shirt and tie, ready to go, and let's get started."

I was in. My life had begun.


## STANDING OUT FROM THE REST

At this point, I've made it abundantly clear that it's not how you settle in your life, but how you **fight** for your life, even if you **face** misfortune, even if you face something that's impossible to overcome.

Or seemingly impossible at the time.

This is the moment where you look at my story and see yourself. You can see how I am just another person, without any superpowers, and yet, I stepped into my life.

I did this by separating myself from everyone else.

The **law of separation** is critical, regardless of where you are in your life. Simply stated, you must separate yourself from the pack, from the competition.

In every situation there is always a group of people who will do just well enough. And because of that, there is a huge opportunity for you. Every time there is a chance to **shore up the gaps in activity or production** that are not getting done by the rest of the group, that is your opportunity to fill in and give more service rendered than wage compensated.

Most people in life focus on what they're going to get out of life versus what they can *give to life*.

Emerson's Law of Compensation is a very similar principle. The main premise is that you give more than you immediately get back with the understanding that, later, you *receive in abundance*.

I applied this law, as I moved up the ladder in the automotive industry, and reaped the opportunity to become a partner in a car dealership at thirty-five years of age.

Separate yourself to stand out – and get noticed. Yes, it seems scary, but when you have faith and a direction, you can do it.

And then you can celebrate your success.


# SHIFTING GEARS: A NEW DIRECTION

When you think about the word "direction", what does that mean to you? Are you taking your career, right now, in the direction you desire? Your *direction = your destination*. You can't pack up the mini-van with all the sunscreen, towels, beach balls and drinks headed to Miami to enjoy the beach if you jump on I-95 North heading towards New York. Direction is critical if you want to arrive at your destination.

What is your hope for your future?

And how about your marriage, other relationships or maybe how you are raising your children?

These are questions I don't have to ask you or remind you of, as everyone considers them every single day.

True, they may not be the same questions, and they may not come to the same answers as you do, but humans are always thinking. We're always thinking about what happens next.

You know my story and you know how I ended up where I was, but this is only a part of what I want to show you. In addition, I want to show you how to drive your life into the sunset, into the happy place where you get what you want.

Where you have what you need.

Where you are truly happy and content.

To get to that place, you need to start putting these lessons into action. You need to start focusing on what your purpose is, even if you don't know how to name it just yet.

# THE POWER OF PURPOSE

*"God is a God of purpose!"* ~ Myles Monroe

Finding **purpose** in life is such a critical component of **understanding** the direction in which you are going.

When you hear that, doesn't it make perfect sense?

Generally in life, so many people are kind of like Alice in Wonderland. In the story, Alice eventually learns about the importance of knowing what she wants, or purpose. And she continues to ask people until she comes to her own answer.

And she wakes up where she realizes she should have been all along – in a place that was happy, content, and safe.

We can learn a great deal about the importance of the power of purpose and goals from her conversation with the Cheshire Cat.

At a critical point, Alice asks the cat, "Would you tell me, please, which way I ought to go from here?"

"That depends a good deal on where you want to get to," said the Cat.

"I don't much care where," said Alice.

"Then it doesn't matter which way you go," said the Cat.

I think you get my point.

I've spent a lot of time talking to kids of all ages in assemblies, chapels, services, and colleges. No matter where I have spoken, I continue to be amazed by how people of all ages have no idea what to do or what their purpose might be.

They're dumbfounded, possibly by all the choices, but also by the outside pressure of what 'success' is supposed to look like.

Think about it. If I had stuck to what success was supposed to look like in my life, and then I didn't get it, I would have ended up miserable. I would have stayed at Chili's and Lowe's.

I would have given up.

Okay, if you're fifteen and don't have a purpose in mind, that is understandable, but when you're forty-five and have no purpose, that is unacceptable.

Even though this sounds a little harsh, you know it's the truth.

It has been said that there are two great days in a person's life – the first is the day they were born, the second is the day they know why they were born. It is all about **purpose**.

Once you understand what you are here for and what you want to accomplish as a definite major purpose of life, everything you do should be wrapped around that purpose.

What are you here for?

What gets you up in the morning?

What keeps you going when things get tough?

When you can answer those questions, you will uncover your purpose and you will begin to understand why you are here.

## YOUR MIND MATTERS IN THIS SEARCH

Psychologists and behavioral scientists have discovered that whatever the mind can conceive and believe, it can achieve.

Let's look back at Napoleon Hill's "Think and Grow Rich" as a phenomenal resource for finding out how your mind matters.

If you don't want to read it right now, here's what you need to know: your ***mind controls everything***. When you can set your mind in the right direction, your actions and your success will follow.

That's it. Really.

It doesn't matter your education or your background. When looking at Thomas Edison's life and all the discoveries he made, you should know that he had only ***three months*** of formal education in his life.

It doesn't matter how many failed attempts you have had in the past. Truthfully, you can write your own price tag in life if you are ready to receive it. But you have to know where you are going.

And you can only know where you are truly meant to go when you uncover your true, unique purpose.

The Lord has given you complete and undivided control over your mind, your thinking, and your brain. That is it.

He didn't give you control over the weather. He didn't give you control over your kids' reactions.

He didn't give you control when the sun rises or sets. He didn't give you control of the seasons. You can't request two summers, one spring and no winters.

He didn't give you control over your spouse, nor did He give you control over your boss.

The power you have to **control your thoughts** is greater than poverty, greater than fear, and greater than lack of education. This power is a gift from God, and He gave this gift to every human being.

Whenever you speak of the things you don't want in life, you are speaking those very same things into existence. You are attracting the very thing to you that you say you don't want. The exciting thing is, however, when you speak positive things of definite purpose, and you control those thoughts, you can bring those concepts or events to yourself, as well.

Try this test.

Gather five of your closest friends and ask them, "What do you want to do in the next five years of your life?"

Watch how two or three of them will tell you what **they don't want** in their life in the next three to five years. Look at the people who talk about what they do want. They're the ones to watch and the ones to share ideas with, since they already know where your mind goes, your life goes.

(Actually, this is much like keeping your eyes on a certain part of the road when you drive. Wherever your attention goes, your action goes, and often swerving off in that direction when you're in a car!)

71

Energy and action *ALWAYS follow thought!* What are you thinking?

You have to intentionally change your focus to your purpose, your definite purpose. You must set your navigation and go in that direction. Your brain is like a mental GPS. It will take you exactly where you program it to take you.

"As a man thinks in his heart, so is he." (Proverbs 23:7). All success begins with a definite purpose.

## NAMING YOUR DEFINITE PURPOSE

Definite purpose is what you intend to get or to be: success, money, love, or basically anything you are, for certain, committed to achieving.

Definite purpose can be used in either a constructive way (to bring to you what you desire) or destructive way (to bring to you what you do not desire), depending on how a person uses it.

Definite purpose must be backed with a plan. It is not important that the plan is perfect, as adjustments are often necessary along the way, but changes can be made if the plan is unsound.

Get a piece of paper and write down your definite purpose, what you plan on giving in return, and the date by which you plan to attain it.

When you have written the statement, read it a minimum of *twice each day*, once when you wake up and again before sleeping at night. Go the next step and record that statement to your phone. *Listen to it daily*. I like to say *Ink it don't think it*. There is power in writing it down, re-reading it daily, and listening to yourself on a recording. I know this may sound silly, however, we all have self-talk. Have the conversation with yourself daily about what you want, not about what you don't want.

If you follow these simple steps, you will start to notice that your desire to attain your definite purpose will attract to you people that have similar desires as you.

I know of many who have started their own business by following this first step. Most of these achievers have read their purpose aloud a minimum of three times a day.

To reinvent yourself, you must create a mental picture so your mind has a clear idea of what you want. You might even choose something that's so big it's considered crazy. If you can see it in your mind, you can hold it in your hand.

By way of example, I have always wanted to buy the Miami Dolphins. I've been saying that since I was twenty. Being a big Dolphins fan, that is exciting and motivating, and it's a big goal. Some people think I'm crazy, but why not focus on a big goal anyway?

You're not crazy. You're just trusting your mind to figure out how to get from where you are to where you want to be (Proverbs 3:5).

Napoleon Hill uses an interesting metaphor. When you are born, you bring with you into life two sealed envelopes. Envelope number one says that you can have anything you wish in life so long as you direct your mind toward that which you want.

The second envelope says that failure is the penalty you must pay by not taking responsibility for the thoughts in your mind.

When you think about that, it sounds basic. You have to set your course and you have to have a purpose. If you don't control your thoughts, someone else ends up steering your ship. Embrace the contents that are in that first envelope. Remember the blessings you get for controlling those thoughts: peace of mind, freedom from fear and worry, and a positive mental attitude. You can enjoy good health and even material items if that is what you desire, but if you don't control your thoughts, the price you pay includes fear, worry, indecision, procrastination, and discouragement.

The ups and downs, poverty, and even ill health are often things that result from a lack of definite purpose.

The second envelope is not the one you want to open, folks.

But if you don't control your thoughts this is the envelope you will end up opening. So how do you do it?

## HOW TO DEFINE YOUR PURPOSE TODAY

I like step-by-step action plans. They're easier to follow and they allow me to know when I've gotten to a certain point.

So, here's what I've come up with your purpose process:

Action 1: Write down your life goal, your purpose in life.
This is not about a one-year goal or a three-year goal. It is not even about your ten-year goal. This is a purpose for your entire life.

If you could have it your way and have everything you wanted, what would be the one thing you would write down as your purpose? What you want to do is begin with the end in mind and back yourself up to where you are now.

You will have one-year goals and three-year goals, but you must start with your purpose. Think about creating a big vision with small steps.

Action 2: Ask yourself, what do I intend to give for what I want?
Giving is a huge component of receiving. You can't take, take, and take your whole life. The only way you receive is you must first give.

There is no lottery ticket; there is no something-for-nothing.

So, if you have a big dream, a big purpose, a big goal or something huge in mind, what price are you willing to pay?

Action 3: Memorize your definite purpose and read or listen to it two or three times daily.
You can put it on CD or record it on your phone; you can write it before you go to sleep or when you wake up the next morning or you can read it aloud.

The point is you want to make sure you have it memorized. If someone were to ask you what your purpose in life is, you can, without a shadow of hesitation or doubt, clearly communicate it.

Here's a quick jumpstart program to finding your definite purpose.
Think about what you will achieve over the next ninety days. Write it down together with steps that you will take to achieve it.

Imagine specifically what you will see, feel, and hear as you achieve your goal.

Think about it until you can run a mental movie of what you want over and over again. In particular, think about how achieving your goal will make you feel, and build the intensity of that emotion in your mind.

## MANUFACTURER RECOMMENDATIONS

#1 – Question Your Direction and Gain Understanding
There are no accidents or coincidences in life. Developing understanding is vital to your growth and success in life. How do you gain understanding in your life?

Realize the end of something is just the beginning of something else. Learn to love being uncomfortable. Growth takes place more rapidly in the uncomfortable or panic zone. Put yourself in position to be uncomfortable as often as possible.

Will you create a positive outlook on your current situation, realizing that it is for your success or growth?

_____

_____

_____

_____

How can you build on your new or current situation?

_____

_____

_____

_____

#2 – Knowing and Applying the Laws
Can you apply the Law of Separation to your situation?

_____

_____

_____

_____

Is there more information available for you to acquire for your situation? If so, what?

_____

_____

_____

_____

It's not where you start but where you finish that's important. Your focus is key. What new focus can you have about your current situation that will contribute to a strong finish?

_____

_____

_____

_____

What two laws can you now apply?

1. _____

2. _____

Do you see value in Emerson's Law of Compensation, to always give more than you are compensated for?

_____

_____

_____

_____

_____

## #3 – Name It

What do you want in your life? Right now, regardless of your age. If you had it, how would it change your life? Write down what you want.

_____

_____

_____

_____

_____

Write down how it would change your life.

_____

_____

_____

_____

_____

How would you feel if you had it? Be descriptive of how it feels.

_____

_____

_____

_____

_____

What price are you willing to pay to get it?

_____

_____

_____

_____

_____

What will you give of yourself (emotionally, spiritually, physically) to attain it?

_____

_____

_____

_____

_____

You must be willing to give more of yourself than you should to accomplish the purpose. Are you willing to write it down, memorize it, live and breathe it to attain it? Are you willing to commit your life for it? Promise yourself that you will by writing out the promise to yourself on the lines below.

_____

_____

_____

_____

_____

# 5 - TUNE UP TIME(S)

*"You have to be able to see in the dark what your
Creator told you in the light." ~ Eric Thomas*

It's all positive thoughts so far, isn't it? The more you place your mind in the direction of your dreams, the more likely you will get to where you want to go.

But even the most positive mind will take detours.

Things aren't always clear, and things are sometimes muddied, or things just change because you change as a person.

In these times, you need to tune things up.

## ARE YOU BLIND?

Look into the future fifty years from now, envision your life in front of you, exactly as you want it, then work your way backward to your current position.

To have **vision** is to begin with the end in mind, seeing the end result before it actualizes, and seeing the invisible. Vision is a powerful principle of success.

So, how well can you see? And how good are your glasses?

*Being blind and having no vision* are two entirely different things. It is essential that you develop a vision for your life.

If I would show you a bag of seeds in an envelope, and they were labeled 'Apple,' most of you would say those are apple seeds. Still, someone out there with vision might say they are apple trees, or even further, an orchard of apple trees.

Now that's vision!

Having a mental picture of a future state, the power to envision what is possible to happen, is what generates success.

Every great accomplishment starts with a clear vision. Once you have a clear vision, you can then take intelligent action. Acting without a vision is generally a waste of time, resources, and energy.

Let's use a relatable example for most.

Can you have a great marriage without a clear understanding of what a great marriage is? Rarely to never. If you do not have clarity to lead you forward, you wander in a state of fog, unable to stay the course when times are difficult.

Consider Walt Disney World, Las Vegas, downtown Miami, or South Beach on Ocean Drive and 7th Street. Someone had to come up with that purpose, someone had to create that vision, someone had to see, not a desert, but the lights of Las Vegas and the magic of Disney World before they were ever created. And your life, your career, your relationships, and your marriage are no different.

When I was twenty years old and started to sell cars, I had no vision for my business, my marriage, or myself. But when I understood what I could achieve in the business, my creative juices started flowing, and at twenty-two years of age, I had a vision of being a sales manager.

I started to grow my vision and I realized that I could not only excel, but also become a general manager of a car dealership. As I continued to grow in my understanding of how the business worked in relation to customers, I knew it could be done better. Therefore, I had to own a car dealership. ***I created the mental picture***.

In my mind's eye, I began to envision: Louie Herron Toyota. It was absurd, right?

At that time *I didn't know when or how* (Proverbs 3:5) in the world I would, or even could, obtain that goal.

I looked out at my life fifty years down the road and realized that I had, in my vision, bought the Miami Dolphins at sixty-five. I started doing the math as to how this could be accomplished.

I created a plan for success, which included goal writing, affirmations, prayer, reading, and more information gathering.

It must become an M.O. or Magnificent Obsession.

No matter who you are, you can have an M.O. You don't have to be rich or powerful to develop a Magnificent Obsession and no down payment is required. (It's free!) Begin right where you are by writing a goal and casting a vision.

*"Vision without action is a daydream. Action without vision is a nightmare."*

To understand what you want and believe that you can attain it is more important than the plan.

Back in 2002, I was a General Sales Manager for a Honda dealership in Atlanta, Georgia. Because it was what I had claimed in my vision, I knew it was going to be done. It had become my Magnificent Obsession.

I knew I was going to be a GM. In fact, I knew I was going to be a GM by the time I was twenty-eight years old because that is what I had written down.

I had followed all the principles I'm sharing with you. I also requested that corporate facilitate circumstances to allow me to go to the NADA (National Automotive Dealers Association) dealer academy.

Remember, at that time I wasn't even a general manager, let alone an owner of a car dealership. But I had asked them to contribute financially for the training, so that when I became a GM, I would be well prepared.

***I would rather be prepared with no opportunity, than have an opportunity and not be prepared.***

Spoiler alert: They turned down my request.

I had a decision to make.

Do I go to the training and pay for it myself?

OR

Do I hope maybe it will just come to pass?

The reality is that I barely had the money it cost: $15,000. But I paid for that training myself, every penny of it. I was not even a general manager yet, and I wanted to spend $15,000 for something that I had no guarantee of having. My wife at the time and I had a few intense conversations on the subject, to say the least. But she saw something in me and believed in me. She gave me her support.

What I'm saying to you is that you must take the necessary steps; sometimes even doing something that **seems irrational**.

Put forth the effort, go against the grain and sell everyone that is involved in the process to help you get to where you have to go.

Believe me, what you think about is what you bring about. That includes all the plans, strategies, people, and even resources. Whether you can understand this principle or not, it works.

You make the vision and then the vision makes you. Making an investment in yourself is time and sometimes money. Money that you don't have? You may say I can't afford to in-vest in myself. I say you can't afford NOT to invest in yourself! Life is risky. Investing money is risky, not investing money is risky. Taking a chance is risky, not taking a chance is risky. You get the point...Life is risky.

Take the risk, you can't afford not to. Your life and future depend on it.

# WHO HAS TIME FOR GOALS?

If you are going to live through the struggle and come out on top, you must understand the power of *goal setting*. But in this world we live in, who has time for goals?

Who has time to commit to the process it takes to think this through and record it? To write down on a piece of paper your one-year, three-year, five-year and even your ten-year goals?

I have chosen not to repackage great goal-setting ideas that I may have heard from other people. I'm strictly referring to my own experiences with goals, which I have been writing down since I was eighteen years of age.

What I have learned is that seeing value in goals and believing in them is the key. I am utterly convinced that you must truly believe before you become.

*You must believe before you can become.*

Why should I set my goals in writing?

- Goals keep you excited.

- Goals give purpose to your activity.

- Goals make you think.

- Goals make you visualize how you want those things.

- Goals get/keep you focused on results.

- Goals teach you to pay attention and pay the price.

- Goals keep you on task.

- Goals keep you working hard with purpose.

- Goals help you make a good plan and drive you to do the little things that make big differences.

I'll show you some of the goals I wrote down in 1998. They are as follows:

- I will be a general manager by the time I am 28 years old.

- I will own a dealership by the time I am 35 years old.

- I will own three dealerships before I am 41 (missed this one).

- I will do public speaking at least three times a year to help and benefit young people.

- I am an incredible dad.

These are just a few examples of some past and present goals.

True, they are simple goals, as within each one there are many more details than just the statements. However, I want you to focus on how I wrote down each goal statement.

Written in present form, it is, 'I will' and 'I am,' not 'I'll try' or 'I might.'

It is written with certainty, confidently claiming the goal as already having been accomplished. Goal setting requires some **faith**.

Notice also, that there is a definite date by which those goals will be accomplished. A goal is a dream with a deadline. Deadlines keep you focused and working hard with purpose.

From this list of goals I just shared, all have been accomplished with the exception of owning three dealerships before I'm forty-one. I'm forty-two now as of this writing and missed a few of my goals. Does that mean I failed? Just because I failed doesn't make me a failure and the same goes for you. Regroup, rewrite, and redo! Always move forward.

Mental action must become paper action, and then paper action must become proper action.

When goals are in your head, they are just wishes or dreams, but when you put them on paper, this action has concreteness to it, and becomes part of the realm of reality. Remember **"Ink it, don't think it."**

Let me give you an example.

In 1998, I wrote down the goal that I would be a general manager by the time I was twenty-eight years old; at the time I was only twenty-four. Most of my friends and other people who knew about this goal told me, "Wow. That is a pretty lofty goal."

I heard again and again about how unrealistic my goals were. Remember, haters never shoot from the top. You will always have naysayers (a person who habitually expresses negative or pessimistic views).

I turned twenty-eight years old on February 25th. It was February 1st, and the general manager I was working for got promoted to oversee two or three other dealerships on the other side of town.

I thought, *Here's my opportunity*.

I was currently the general sales manager, so the very natural progression was for me to move into the GM position.

86

Unfortunately, the corporate executives felt I was not ready, that I was not the right one for the job. How could a twenty-eight year old kid operate one of the dealer groups largest Honda dealerships in Atlanta, GA (here we go again)?

I had been the general sales manager for the previous three years for this dealership. I was ready. The move was perfect, and the timing was perfect.

I had paid my own tuition to National Automotive Dealership Association Dealer Academy (NADA), so I was trained. I already had some experience and understanding of what it would be like at this next level.

Yet because of my age and because it was a large publicly held company, they felt like there was someone else in Tennessee more qualified than I was at the time (by the way he was more qualified with his years of experience). So that was it.

Where most people would think it was not going to happen, I had this goal written down and I knew it could happen by the time I was twenty-eight, though I admit to ***feeling discouraged***.

I contemplated how I was going to get this position in twenty-five days, as they had already announced the new GM. But I didn't worry. I chose a good attitude, went on with life, and realized that it was possible that it was not my time.

As fate (some would say LUCK, or laboring under correct knowledge) would have it, it was not over.

(Luck is preparation meeting opportunity.)

This is the "work while you wait" philosophy! Keep working and grinding as if you will get the opportunity, and the opportunity will come.

The gentleman from Tennessee elected not to accept the position, as his wife didn't want to move to Atlanta. ***Suddenly the*** *situation changed* and the dealership needed a general manager, literally ten days away from my birthday.

Over the phone, I was told that they were still looking for someone to fill the position, but they were going to name me the *interim general manager*. I was elated. By the way, I ended up keeping the general manager position for three years before they fired me due to "performance". That's a whole 'nother story, but just know I kept on fighting. All I can say is the guy who replaced me didn't stay employed long as well, and I went on to better things. The firing or demotion was a *gift from God*. Only looking back did I realize it was a gift.

Without great detail, I can tell you that I wanted to own a dealership by the time I was thirty-five, and the same scenario played out.

I wasn't as fortunate to get this one prior to my birthday, but by June 15, 2009 (I was still thirty-five), I bought my first dealership.

Prior to this purchase, I was searching and seeking. There was no open door for a dealership of my own. **But for preparation to meet opportunity, you stay prepared, you maintain your vision, you have definite purpose, and you speak your written goal. You are then positioned for things to just happen.**

Is this starting to come together for you? This is how it happens every time. With written goals which you read at least two times a day, rewrite one time a month, record on a CD, record it to your phone and play it in a car five to ten minutes a day, good things just start happening. A lot of people call it the law of attraction.

Whatever you call it, it is real, it is directive, and it works. You can trust me on this one.

## MANUFACTURER RECOMMENDATIONS

#1 – What Do You Want?

Is there something you want so badly in life that you can taste it? What is it? Write down your vision – the one you see for yourself.

List two ways you can use your vision to create an obsession.

1. _____

2. _____

# 6 - SHIFTING INTO GEAR

*"Dreams don't work unless you do."* ~ Peter Daniels

We know that we need to do something, but it's the 'something' that can become confusing, disorienting, and even disappointing.

But we're human and we don't always want to change from what we know. However, if you want to set your life on fire, you need to make sure you're not just talking the talk.

You also need to walk the walk.

## PUTTING GOALS INTO ACTION

Plans in progress release **power**. We've already talked about writing your goals down on paper, but if you haven't done it already, stop what you're doing and complete the task.

From there, we also want to think about the things you've already done and the things you've already accomplished. Believe it or not, you've already been successful in your life, even if you don't realize it.

You've already made things happen that were amazing – even if you didn't notice it at the time.

Write down five things you have accomplished in your life, things you are proud of and things you are happy to say you did.

You want to start there because it is important to start with **gratitude**. Not only does this remind you of your own ability to change your life and to create things you want, but it also brings your mind into a space of gratitude, which is a positive space.

When you're positive, you can make things happen.

This step will give you momentum as you move into your dreams and into your purpose in life. In fact, it's helpful to write out all of the things for which you are ***grateful*** as often as you can.

The more you do it, the more you can set your mind on being positive about what's happening right now. After all, would it have helped me to continue to focus on how bad my job was at Chili's? What would that have achieved?

What it probably would have done is made me bitter about my choices, and less excited about the choices I made after that.

Instead, let's try something new. A key to getting more in life is to be ***grateful*** for what you already have. If you're always looking at what ELSE you might want, you're not being thankful.

You're overlooking opportunities to be ***grateful***.

When you can open up to gratitude, you can open up your life and create space for more things to happen. After all, you're then putting out the energy that you're ***grateful*** for what you have now, and everything else that is to come would also receive that same gratitude.

Consider what it is that you want in the next ten years and write it down. I'm not referring to what you think you can get, or if everything works out. Write down what you want to have happen in the next ten years.

Write down what WILL happen in the next ten years, as if you can already see into the future.

As if you already know.

For some, this might not be an exciting step to take. You might struggle with this step, but I want you to push forward anyway. Turn on some happy music and slip into your comfy clothes and enjoy this process.

# DRIVEN BY F.I.R.E.

Write down fifty specific things that you want in the next ten years. Be bold! Write down the things you want to have, **even if you're not quite sure how they might happen** – and write them down even if you don't believe you can have them all.

You can. But you need to name them first.

These fifty items can revolve around lifestyle, houses, automobiles, jewelry, or other material items. You might also focus on your personal development goals. Here are some questions for you to ponder as you begin to make your special list:

- What do you see yourself becoming or what do you want to do?

- What are things you want to do in the community?

- What do you want to do in your church?

- What do you want to do in your life?

- Where do you want to go and with whom do you want to spend your time?

- Do you want to visit another country? What country do you want to visit and with whom do you want to go?

- How about debt goals? What things do you want to eliminate?

- What things do you want out of your life?

Once you have this life 'wish list', start to break things down more.

Every single goal should be classified into specific categories assigned to them: spiritual, financial, emotional, physical, relational, family, travel, etc.

(And while I've written down 100 things, you can start with fifty and see how that works for you.)

Once you have written down the fifty items, give each one a number based on when you think you can achieve it. A one means one year, three stands for three years, etc.

This allows you to connect your goals to time frames. After completing the time frames, sort all fifty items into lists by one-year, three-year, five-year and ten-year categories.

See how many you have in each category.

Now, all of this might seem like a lot of **work**, but what you're actually doing is creating more substance for your life. You're stopping the busy-ness of your life to think about what you actually want.

You've also just determined which goals have a higher priority than others. For some, getting debt out of the way is a goal before traveling to Europe.

For others, those priorities might be switched.

I'm not here to tell you there is a right or a wrong way to take on this task, just the way that works best for you.

Once you have these established and recorded, go back and rewrite the goals with a deadline. Be specific with the date.

Write each goal you stated in a current, or achieved, format – 'I will,' not 'I want,' not 'I would like to,' not 'I think.'

The following are examples:

- I will have my debt paid off in 2016.

- I will learn how to fly a plane in 2016.

Here's where your technology will come in handy too.

Take out your smartphone or some other recording device.

Read all of the goals you've written down with the deadlines and the positive intentions. Read those goals into your recording device. You might want to create different recordings for each of the different time frames, or you might put them all on one recording, starting with the one-year goals first.

Then, listen to the recordings.

Listen to each of the recordings for about five minutes a day. That's all it takes to get started. Over time, you might want to double that listening time to ten minutes a day – or more.

Make sure you keep your goals in written form as well. You can further put these goals into your consciousness by reading them in the morning when you awake and read them at night when you go to bed.

Finally, rewrite your same goals once a month. This doesn't mean you need to make new goals (though that might be possible). What this does mean is that you will be writing and rewriting your goals twelve times a year.

Your list might change constantly, but you'll always come back to the idea that you are going to reach this set of fifty goals, on your timeline, and by those set deadlines.

No question. No doubt.

*Goal setting* will change your life if you let it. The key is taking everything out of your head and putting it on paper. You don't want just dreams and wishes.

You need goals. You need bold statements of intention.

Knowing my own experience with goal setting, a couple of cautions come to mind: behold and beware.

**'Behold'** would be the positive side of the goal setting process, in which you become aware and take notice of things that are happening. Make sure you stay vigilant and see what is happening around you.

Notice when your goals are becoming reality.

**'Beware'** is negative and this caution speaks more to having an awareness of yourself in the process of reaching your goals.

Are you becoming obsessed? Are you giving up too much to get a goal that may not be as important to you as you thought at first?

Some goals may cost you too dearly. The price may demand too much sacrifice. Be careful of your obsessions. **Don't let them drive you to compromise your virtues or your values.** Let's pause to make sure you understand what I mean by compromise.

In life there are sacrifices. In life there are stages. Pay close attention to what "stage" of life you are in as well as the "sacrifices" you're about to consider. You could be married and your goals are not lining up with your spouse's goals. You MUST be in line together or there WILL be trouble (I've experienced this myself). That stage could be critical to your success. Maybe you have two kids, activities, house chores, quality time with your family. Applying the big "M.O." and not being on the same page with your family could **cost you everything**. Sacrificing your responsibilities as a spouse and parent would not be wise, hence compromising your values and the virtue of your marriage.

# THE POWER OF RENEWING YOUR MIND

*"Success is not something you pursue, it is something you attract. It is attracted to you as you become an attractive person. I have always thought of life as being an inside game with an outside reflection. Simply put, what is in your heart and in your mind comes out of your mouth and body."*

*"As you think in your heart, so are you."* ~ Proverbs 23:7

# DRIVEN BY F.I.R.E.

You've likely heard of the idea that when you put your mind to something, you can do anything. And while this might make sense in some ways, it may not make sense in other ways.

It's just something that you've heard and believed. So what?

Nothing you do, no energy or action, ever comes before thought – even if it's not a conscious thought.

Our brains are always working, even when we're sleeping.

Thought is a crucial part of your success. The only thing that God gave you 100% control of is your thoughts and how you think.

This is why *renewing your mind* is so important to your growth, your success in life, and, more importantly, to how you come out on top in the midst of struggles in your own life.

The graveyard is one of the wealthiest places on the planet because there are so many unrealized dreams, accomplishments, and possibilities that were *never* even attempted in life.

How does this happen? I might suggest that their minds were not renewed.

People are afraid of failing and that fear may have caused them to hold back. On their deathbed, they may have even whispered, "I should have done 'it' anyway."

I have been fired four times in my automotive career. Four times I was told I wasn't good enough. I'm not bragging about it, but it simply doesn't matter. In fact, after every termination I endured, the opportunity I received afterward was better in every way. Do you think the way *I thought* about life with the principles I'm sharing made a difference in my thinking? You better believe it. It made all the difference.

The very last time I was fired was six months before I purchased Louie Herron Toyota. Just six months before buying my own dealership, I wasn't good enough to work for someone else's dealership. How does that work? **Faith, Intensity, Re-inventing yourself, and Enthusiasm.**

It happens. And you may not have any control over it.

But when you renew your mind and you fortify your resolve, you don't have to let these moments stop you.

You don't have to let anyone else tell you that you CAN'T do something.

Not even yourself.

You can move forward and move into the person you were destined to be – and the person who you truly want to be.

The person you already are.

# HOW TO MOVE PAST ADVERSITY

Adversity comes to every person; there are no exceptions.

Even the most successful people, the people you admire most, have faced adversity.

And they have moved past it. They have used it to become stronger and better.

I encourage you to take the attitude that **God is always conspiring for your benefit.**

Have you ever heard of the crab syndrome? This happens the minute you make the decision to stop playing it safe with your life and truly go for what you want. When you do this, when you take the scary step others will not take, there will always be crabs focused on keeping you down in the bucket (haters from the bottom).

They don't want you to change because it means they could change too.

Too many times in life, and you may be in this situation right now, people **run from pain** instead of **running toward gain**. So when you make that decision to go forward, stay focused on what you want.

New attitudes can produce powerful results.

You have probably made fun of people you see walking down the street talking to themselves. But you and I are no different.

The exception is that we quietly have these conversations in our heads. Instead of thinking about whether you talk to yourself or not, consider what you say to yourself day in and day out.

What is the internal dialogue that you play over and over in your mind?

If you could tape those conversations and play them back at the end of the day, would they please you or embarrass you?

Or would you clearly see that the results you are having in your life directly reflect what you say to yourself over and over each day?

Think about what you are saying to yourself. If you had a friend that talked to you the way you talk to yourself, you probably wouldn't have him/her as a friend very long.

A part of renewing your mind means **rewriting your inner conversations**, choosing to speak positive messages to your- self because you want positive energy and actions.

Okay, so this isn't something that will happen quickly or easily.

You've been having these conversations with yourself for the past ten, twenty, maybe even thirty years. Some of the conversations came from within yourself, while others may have come from others: your friends, your family, your peers, your boss, etc.

But you are the one that continues to play back these conversations, even if they didn't come from you to begin with.

You can change what you tell yourself.

You can change what you think about yourself.

You can change your life right now.

## FOUR METHODS OF BRAIN TRAINING

I've been talking a lot about renewing your brain, and now we're going to take action on this suggestion and piece of advice.

I would encourage you to pick out a few of the following methods to try in your own life.

Or just choose one that seems to sound best to you. Over time, you might add another. Or not.

It's up to you.

Affirmation
Affirmations are audible daily validations that you speak to yourself. These are positive statements, or reminders, that you say aloud.

Personally, I repeat my chosen affirmations for 25 or 30 minutes per day, and I know they work. I know they contribute to the positive conversations and outcomes I want for my life.

When I first started doing affirmations, I didn't know why they worked. And they still work. So, you don't have to understand why.

But I later learned about the reticular activating system (RAS) in the brain. When you use the spoken word out loud, your own voice actually creates a feedback loop to yourself.

Take the example of a pregnant woman. She is constantly thinking of her baby. Constantly thinking about newborn concerns. The thoughts consume her daily. Consequently what does she always see? Other pregnant women (RAS) at work, and that's the same concept with constantly thinking positive or negative thoughts. Your brain is doing that now whether you realize it or not.

Your subconscious doesn't care if you are black, white, tall, skinny, female or male. All it does is record the information you give it and attract like conversations right directly to you.

Affirmations are powerful change agents for self-conversations. Imagine what it would be like to hear messages in your brain that tell you how great you are and how successful you will be.

Now that might encourage you to start talking to yourself more often. (And hopefully listen to what you have to say!)

Visualization
Visualization is a technique in which you begin to see things or outcomes with your mind's eye.

It sounds a little New Age-y, and it is, but it also works. Like your brain's process of interpreting affirmations, your brain responds in the same way to your visualizations as it would in real life.

For example, if you visualize yourself with a positive bank account, you will feel happy and your brain will react accordingly.

By training your brain to visualize the outcomes of your goals, your brain will believe these situations to be true. Your whole body and mind will simply begin to accept what you think to be true.

And then it will become true.

Professional athletes use visualization all the time to picture how their perfect game might look. Over and over, they picture their movements in their minds, and then they see the same movements happen during competitions.

Because training your brain works, and it impacts what happens in real life.

Seriously, take the time to sit down and play your mental movie. I have literally sat down in a quiet spot thousands of times and visualized myself in a movie theater. The chairs, the popcorn, etc. and watched my movie play out. It takes a lot of focus, but you are the director of your life (movie).

Memorizing

Whatever has your focus also has you. With this in mind, let your goals dominate your focus.

Memorize and repeat the things you want to see manifested in your life: your goals, your affirmations and your visions.

Doing this will help you put them at the top of your thoughts. Your focus, energy, and actions will always follow your thoughts.

The Prayer of Gratitude

The best way to obtain what you want in life is to be grateful for what you have already. Set aside time to practice expressing gratitude. Pray out loud. Communicate with yourself how grateful you are for your spouse, for your children, for your current job, for your health, etc. If you affirm what you already have, you will gain the ability to attain more.

You now have information that you can apply to your life today. Start off today by changing the negative daily conversation you have with yourself to the positive and uplifting conversation that you want to have.

# MANUFACTURER RECOMMENDATIONS

## #1 – Do The Work

Start writing, start recording, and start memorizing. Put pen to paper and transfer the goal from your head to the page right now.

(If you haven't already.)

Start writing goals out from one to fifty (or more), keeping these categories in mind:

- Financial/debt

- Spiritual

- Lifestyle

- Family

- Relationships

- Weight loss/physical health

- Career

- Emotional

- Material items (cars, homes, vacations, planes, etc.)

Next, make sure you write out the time frames for each goal, and then separate the goals into their time frames.

You'll begin to see your priorities, and you'll begin to see what you need to do next.

## #2 – Affirmations & Outcomes & Prayers

List five affirmations starting with "I am" that you will begin to say to yourself today.

1. _____

2. _____

3. _____

4. _____

5. _____

List five outcomes you will visualize for your life that you will begin to affirm today.

1. _____

2. _____

3. _____

4. _____

5. _____

Write out a specific prayer of gratitude that you will memorize today. Express things from your life for which you are grateful today, and include things from your vision for your future.

_____

_____

_____

_____

_____

# 7 - KEEPING YOUR CAR RUNNING

*"The pessimist sees the difficulty in every opportunity;*
*an optimist sees the opportunity in*
*every difficulty." ~ Winston Churchill*

Once you've put all of these practices into place, and once you've said what you want, you can't sit still. Though you are primed for things to happen around you, you still have to **do the work**.

And from this point forward, your work is staying focused.

Imagine what might happen if you were to stop looking at the road while you were driving. Even one moment of not paying attention can take you from the right path and even be dangerous.

**Your success is the same way**.

## STAY FOCUSED ON THE OUTCOME!

A positive person sees opportunity even in the midst of difficulty. Positive people tend to be FOTO, **Focused On The Outcome**, so they see opportunity in every difficulty.

That kind of focus is at the heart of being successful.

Many people think they are being positive, but they live unexamined lives - they never take the time to find out what is really happening in their lives.

So let's find out how positive you really are.

Look first at the commitments you have in your life.

If you say you want to have a great relationship with your spouse, your children, or even your boss, but what constantly shows up in the conversations you have about those people are things you dislike, then truthfully, you are more committed to the dislikes or the problems of that relationship than to having a great relationship.

***What you are most committed to always shows up.***

## TAKING INVENTORY

Often in business or relationships, or in life, we tend to focus on the 20% that is frustrating or bad, while we ignore the 80% that is going great.

Knowing this, think about an issue that has been bothering you. Take inventory of what is also going well. Write down everything positive about that issue. When you have exhausted every possible positive you can think of, make a second list of the negatives of the issue.

This practice allows you to focus on what is right and what you have to be grateful for, even when things aren't 100% perfect. Nothing will be perfect! Your expectations of perfection will stall or paralyze your forward movement.

If your list of positives doesn't outweigh the negatives, then you have identified some areas in which you can take action to secure change.

***Change*** is inevitable in life, but ***growth*** is always optional.

Stephen Covey confirms this advice in his classic book, *The Seven Habits of Highly Effective People*. It harkens back to our section on vision as he says, "Begin with the end in mind."

One other issue to highlight in this 'inventory' section is specific language in your goals. If you have a goal that is too broad, not outcome specific, then the likelihood of accomplishing that goal is very slim.

For example, in the sales business we talk about the goal of making more calls. Unfortunately, making more calls is not specific enough; there is no accountability in just making more calls.

Better language would be, "I will make twenty calls a day and for thirty days straight."

That is specific and measurable, and leads to an outcome.

Many goals are never reached because they are not SMART (Specific, Measurable, Attainable, Relevant and Timed).

Consider right now your goals and how you might make them SMART too.


## FOCUSING ON OUTCOME

The outcome is what you are after, but the **process** is more important than the product.

No excuses. No alibis. No quitting.

When challenging circumstances arise, and **they always will**, look for new resources with which to accomplish your goal. Don't look for more excuses that support the new circum-stances. An excuse will NEVER better your situation.

The car business is very competitive and the manufacturers like Chrysler, Dodge, Jeep, Ram, Ford, Honda, Toyota, etc., are always looking for increased market share. They place dealer-ships in specific geographical locations to maximize brand loy-alty and brand market share.

Therefore, if my dealership is supposed to attain 13% market share, and my goal is 25% market share, how can I attain an increased market share of 12% if there are only so many peo-ple in the marketplace?

Remember, having only so many people in the marketplace is just a circumstance.

You have to be 'unreasonable' and you have to use 'unreasonable' resources to get what you want.

So I ask you these questions:

- When was the last time you thought in an 'unreasonable' manner?

- When was the last time you set an outcome that most others said could not be done?

- When was the last time circumstances showed up, and you caved in to them?

In the hypothetical illustration about the car industry, if the car industry's share in the market share is only so big, then my only option is to go create a whole new market that's hungry for what I have to offer.

When you are focused on your outcome, the **solution will always show up**. If you are focused on the problems, they will also continue to show up and hinder your progress.

What you are most focused on or committed to will always show up. **Your greatest energy is always created by your clearest focus**. So the more clearly you define your goal, the greater the energy you have.

As you stay positive and outcome-focused, you have the greatest chance for success.


## MANUFACTURERS RECOMMENDATIONS

### #1 - Regroup
Here is where the rubber hits the road. Remember what you're most committed to will show up most often. What I

am committed to is to do this work like no one else, so some day YOU can work like no one else.

Regroup. Stop looking for all the reasons why you can't do something, and reframe the picture to reveal all the reasons why you want to do it. You don't 'have' to do this stuff - you 'get' to do this stuff!

An accomplished goal brings deep satisfaction.

- Write down your goals.

- Put them on a CD.

- Re-write your goals monthly.

- Memorize what you are grateful for.

- Visualize your goals as completed.

- Record to your phone and listen to affirmations.

- Work, don't just wish.

- Cultivate positivity in every way.

Write down three specific outcomes that you will set for yourself over the next 90 days.

1. _____

2. _____

3. _____

# FINAL THOUGHTS . . .

*"If you can dream it, you can do it." ~ Walt Disney*

It's freeing to know that you are in control of your life. It's freeing to know that you're not someone who needs to be controlled by circumstances or someone who has to settle for second best.

If you **believe** that you **deserve** more, you will **get** more.

But this also comes with a bigger question: what will you do now?

## WHAT WILL YOU DO?

From now on, your whole life will be a series of decision points.

Some will not be life altering as 'where will I live?' or 'should I start my diet on Monday?'

However, the decision of **how you will live your life** is a huge choice. You already know this. The problem or opportunity is that decisions must be dealt with every time you get new information to change how you're living.

Success in all areas of your life is very intentional. Regardless of goals and dreams, big or small, to achieve them requires intention, attention, and focus.

- What is your intention now that you have this 'new' information?

- What do you choose to give your attention to?

- How will you remain focused?

- How will you handle adversity, struggles, and circumstances?

Your answers to these questions will create the happiness in your life.

When I think about adversity and struggles, I can't help but think of Michael Jordan who, after being cut from his high school basketball team, went home, locked himself in his room and cried.

Or maybe you can think about Eminem, a high school dropout whose personal struggles with drugs and poverty culminated in an unsuccessful suicide attempt.

Or Steve Jobs. At thirty years of age, he was left devastated and depressed after being unceremoniously removed from the company he had started.

How about Walt Disney who was fired from a newspaper for 'lacking imagination' and for 'having no original ideas'?

The list goes on and on.

There is a huge gap in most people's lives between *'knowing'* and *'doing.'*

That gap can be filled up by you, and you have to do the things outlined in this book to achieve any high level of success in your life.

It doesn't matter to me if you are thirteen or sixty-three, these principles will impact your outcomes. But now the **work** is up to you.

I told you portions of my story to illustrate some of them, but the fact is that we all have the **same story**. It just plays out on different street corners, in different states, through different time frames or in different communities.

People who don't really know me see the outcomes, but have no idea of the story. And if you think about it, they don't know you or your story!

So what if your life is tough right now? So what, life is tough and this too will pass. My deepest held opinion is that the biggest, most influential decision you can make in winning the game of life is the decision to have a relationship with Jesus Christ.

The playing field of life and how you play the game is all about getting to the 'real' finish line. When that day comes, the Lord will ask each of us (no one will be excluded) two questions.

The first is, **"Why should I let you into the gates of heaven?"** and the second is, **"What did you do with what I gave you?"**

God made you to be extraordinary not ordinary, but therein is a choice that only you can make.

Will you move beyond ordinary or not?

God provides the rain. He also provides the sunlight, the soil and the seed. All you have to do is plant the seed. You must do the work. There is no other alternative.

What will you do? That is the question. Will you **shelf** this book or will you **plant** the seed?

People talk about 'the secrets to success' or the 'blueprint for success,' but please understand that success is usually dressed in overalls and resembles nothing more than **work**.

Purpose, vision, goals, renewing your mind, affirmations, and visualizations are all part of the work it takes to achieve a level of success in any area of your life, be it educational, marital, financial, health, etc.

Success is not that common; that's why it is hard for the 'common' man to enjoy it.

## DRIVEN BY F.I.R.E.

There is a big difference between working 'on' your life and working 'in' your life. Circumstances of your life can change, but you have to change yourself to see different results.

Be uncommon today.

Be uncommon now.

Go to work and plant your seed.

# SET YOUR LIFE ON FIRE TODAY: WHAT HAPPENS NEXT

With all of this information, you might not know what happens next. Even if you followed all of the exercises, did all the work, and are raring to go, you might be nervous about the next step.

Breathe for a minute and let's look back at the title of this book because therein lies all of the answers.

You already know how to change your mind and focus your intention and attention, and now it's time to do what you say you'll do.

It's time to make the life that matters to you – and to those around you.

Don't stop now.

# FAITH

From this point on, no more excuses. No more wavering on what you want from your life and no more rationalizations (rational-lies) about how you don't know where to start.

We know what it means to rationalize something, how we rationalize our past lives and our past actions – and we definitely know how to rationalize the lies we've told ourselves.

You have the tools now. You have the ways that will work to help you move forward in your life – to the life you deserve, to the life that's been waiting for you to arrive.

You just need to turn on your faith.

Now, for those of you who are Christians like I am, you already have a sense of what this means. And it's not easy. And it's not going to ever be simple.

Faith is a continuous practice of reaffirming what you believe in. I could go on all day about what I think you should think, but let's expand the idea of faith.

I don't want to leave anyone out when it comes to setting their life on fire.

You just need to have faith in something bigger than yourself. You need to have faith that there is a bigger picture and a bigger story that's taking place.

You need to believe that all of these powers, or God, or whatever you might call this bigger thing, is working in your favor.

It's not a question of what your exact definition of faith or a higher power is, really, that's something that's important to me, but it may not be the driving force for you.

But what if you've forgotten what faith is. That's really simple to do.

Haven't we all had times when we were tested in our lives? One thing went wrong, then another, then another, and before we knew it, our lives blew up in our faces.

***A testing always becomes a testimony***, a story for you to share with others – for others to grow. Testing becomes a blessing.

And we didn't know what to do. We didn't think anything was going to get better. And we were certain that we were going to have the worst luck from that point forward.

We lost faith in life.

We lost faith in ourselves.

We gave up.

This happens to EVERYONE. Truly. There are days when Oprah questions herself and there are days when even the Pope wonders what he's doing and if he's doing it right.

There is nothing wrong with having a few crises of faith.

But you need to get it back NOW. If you're not able to have faith in yourself or faith in something bigger than yourself, you're not going to get far with the rest of your life.

At some point, you just have to have faith in life to turn out the way you want it to turn out – the way it's SUPPOSED to turn out.

## HOW TO TURN YOUR FAITH BACK ON

I have to tell you something right now – there is no magic cure for a loss of faith. I don't have one answer to help every single reader out.

It's not because I haven't tried to think this through either. Trust me; I've lost quite a few nights of sleep trying to give you the answer. But when I prayed about it and when I thought about it, I realized that you need to uncover what your faith is.

I can't tell you what that looks like for you. And if I can't tell you what your faith looks like, I also can't tell you how to bring it back.

Here's what I can tell you, it takes some **work**.

It takes some self-reflection and it takes time to bring yourself back into the place where you have your faith as a partner, not as an adversary.

- Pray – Of course, the first thing I'm going to suggest is that you find moments to pray and to connect with God. This doesn't have to be the biggest prayer you've ever prayed, but you will want to spend time connecting to the voice that's bigger than yours. And even though you might do most of the talking, make sure you're listening as well. You might hear exactly what you need to hear.

- Get outside – When things are awful and you don't know what happens next, get outside of your house and get into nature. There you can find peace and quiet, and you get to be in the company of things that have been around for much longer than you have: trees, stones, mountains, etc. Stop and breathe in the surroundings and the beauty of nature. This is a time when you can focus on the idea that there is more at work than what is happening in your life right at this moment.

- Think bigger – Always go back to the bigger picture when you feel your faith is being tested or it's much less than you thought it was before. Think about things that are bigger than you. Stop thinking so much about the minute-to-minute actions, and think about what the larger moments and lessons of your life have been.

- Go back – Related to this is the suggestion to start looking back at your life like a detective. Look for the times when you thought all was lost, and yet something happened to bring you back to your faith. Focus on those times as reminders that things are never as they seem in the moment. Sometimes, faith is found in the reminders that you have been through horrible things before, and you'll do it again.

The more you **look** for your faith and the more you start to encourage it to reveal itself, the more you will begin to **see** it show up (what you are committed to shows up most often).


## WHEN TIMES ARE TOUGH

Faith is the hardest to remember when times are tough. When everything is going wrong and someone tells you to have faith, you may be tempted to hit them.

So what do you do when everything is going wrong?

- Breathe – When you feel the world closing in on you, stop and take a breath. Then take another. Let things slow down before you react and before you start to lose faith.

- Ask for help – If you are having a hard time, turn to a priest or a minister or a trusted friend. Let them know you need their help, and they can provide you with some light in a dark time. They will remind you that you can always return to faith in those who love you.

- Know that it will get better – Even though you might have to fake this attitude, remember that things will get better. Every day, let yourself hear this phrase again and again. You will eventually believe it because it will happen.

Faith is the first step toward taking what you have learned and putting it into action in your life.

You must believe.

You must believe.


# **INTENSITY**

No matter what you think about sports, you can't argue their intensity. Those who want to be a success put everything into their practices, into their training, and into each game.

They focus on what they want and they do everything possible to make sure they get it.

Everything.

# DRIVEN BY F.I.R.E.

You don't have to be a world-class athlete to see how this can help you too. The more focus you have, the more you will increase your determination and your ability to succeed.

You have to **work** at your life in order to ensure it works for you.

This brings us to the Path Principle. And it's really simple.

Your Attention/Intention = Your Direction = Your Destination.

When you can focus your **intention**, you will go in the right **direction**, which will lead you to the final **destination**.

So, you need to start by finding your attention and your intention.


## GET FOCUSED

You need to get focused when you're setting your life on fire. You need to make sure your heart, your brain, and the rest of your attention is focused only on what you want.

*Everything else is a distraction*.

Since you're probably already excited about what you are doing and what this will mean for your future, you need to re-move anything that is preventing this focus from being as effective as it could be.

- Get rid of distractions – If you were to look at each day, you would find there are many hours that go wasted. You might be on Facebook or doing something else that doesn't support your goals and your desires. So, if you find these distractions in your life, you should get rid of them. Ask yourself, do you want to find success in your life or would you rather watch a TV show? (Note: This answer might vary from day to day, true. However, the more you decide to remove distractions, the easier it will be to reach your goals.)

- Ignore others' opinions – The worst distractions in your life are the people who decide to give you advice. Now, I like advice from others, I really do, but when it starts to interfere with what I'm doing, or it makes me question everything, then it's time to walk away from their best intentions. Instead, think about what you think. Focus on what <u>you</u> want.

- Remind yourself why – To focus on what you want, it's a good idea to remind yourself again and again why you're doing what you're doing. The more you remind yourself, the more you will hang onto the focus you need.

The more you can get and stay focused, the more you will be able to see the results of your hard work and your determination.

You already have the faith you need in yourself, and now you're taking the process even further by eliminating those things that make you question yourself and your path.

## FOCUS VS. OBSESSION

As with anything, you can also become excessive about the focus you have in your life. While I am a strong supporter of being as focused as you can be, if you're not active in your re-lationship, if you're not playing with your children, if you're not doing a great job in your work, etc., you're not doing the rest of your life any favors.

Instead, you need to practice a health focus. This means you still want to remove distractions and start to use more of your attention and energy for your goals, but not at the expense of other things that are important in your life.

- Your family

- Your work obligations

- Your health

Stop and ask yourself frequently if you are still upholding commitments you had before you started this path. If you still are, then proceed. If not, think about whether you need to make changes.

It's not going to be a good idea to have the life you want, but leave others you love behind.

(Unless that's what needs to happen.)

# REINVENTION

Your life might be at the tipping point of changing completely. You may need to completely open up to the possibility that things need to change from the way they have been.

With faith and focus, you will be ready to start seeing things shift before your eyes.

It's often not as exciting as you might think.

Sometimes change comes slowly; so slowly that you may not notice it until it's fully arrived. At other times, change may come suddenly and that suddenness may cause you to push it away.

We are, after all, creatures of habit and we like things to stay the same (even if we say we want things to change).

So, how can you open up to reinvention and invite it in? Faith and focus will get you partly there, but now we need to make sure you're open to what happens next.

Just like on *Extreme Makeover: Home Edition*, think about how Ty Pennington shouts to the driver to "Move that bus!"

You need to shout out to the obstacle(s) in your life to GET OUT OF THE WAY. You can and you will reinvent your life, just like they do in the show.

Maybe it doesn't take a week, but it will happen faster than you think.


## DO YOU NEED TO CHANGE EVERYTHING?

I don't want to generalize everyone's experience, but from what I can tell, change is a scary thing for most people. No matter how much people NEED to change (and they know it), they also want to resist it with just as much fervor.

We don't want to change from what we know because, well, we know what we know. We like what we like, and even though we don't like everything, we're not sure what will happen if we try something new.

I want to let you in on a little secret – little changes are good too. Think of this like a snowball on the side of a mountain. It starts off as this small little piece of frozen water, but as it rolls down the side and collects momentum and snow, it becomes larger and larger.

This metaphor works for life changes too.

Just because you don't change EVERYTHING in your life at the same time doesn't mean you can't make the important shifts that your life needs.

You can start small, and I even encourage you to start small. When you do, you'll find out that change isn't as scary, or you'll find that the 'scary' bit goes away quickly.

You don't have to change everything. That would be absolutely horrible and unsustainable – and, thankfully, unnecessary.

Take **Little steps** until you can't help but take ***bigger steps*** because you know they'll be worth it.

## WHAT TO DO WHEN YOU RESIST CHANGE

At some point, maybe even now, you're going to resist the changes around you. You're going to notice that things feel out of control and you're going to notice you're **scared** and **uncomfortable**.

And you'll be tempted not to do anything else.

You'll be tempted to run back to your old way of living and your old way of being.

I've been there. It'll happen to you too.

When these feelings come up:

Live in the uncertain – Be okay with things not being as you thought they were going to be. When you're changing things up, of course things are going to look and feel different. It's okay to be slightly uneasy once in a while.

Wait it out – When you're trying to change your life, it's best not to make any snap decisions. Instead, think things over for a bit and be okay with not being comfortable all of the time. You might have a period in which change doesn't feel right, but as the days pass, you may change your mind.

Consider what happens next – If you're thinking about going back to the way things were, consider what might happen if you do. Would you be happier? Would you be healthier? Are you making a decision based on **fear** or based on **faith**?

Resistance may be futile, according to some, but it's also going to be present in your experience.

It's how you engage it that makes it your friend or your foe.

# ENTHUSIASM

In the word enthusiasm, you already get a clue about what will happen and what can happen for you:

### *IASM = I AM SOLD MYSELF*

When you're sold, you have enthusiasm. In life you are being sold or selling others. As well as, selling yourself. What are you selling?

Now that you've found faith, intensity, and considered reinvention, how do you keep it up? You get **inspired** (in spirit, getting your flow) and you get **enthusiastic** about the things that are happening around you.

You don't settle for anything less than something that makes you **fired up**!

It's the long-term need to stay fired up that can be the trick for some, so here are some ways to keep yourself up and ready to take on the new day.

## GET INSPIRED (AGAIN AND AGAIN)

You need to stay inspired on your journey because some days, you're not going to see immediate (or any) results. You're going to have moments where you question everything that's happening, and you will have times when you think you're just spinning your wheels.

And sometimes, that might be true.

To keep yourself inspired and ready for action, you need to look to others for inspiration.

Something I like to do is to read inspirational stories about people I admire. I even listed some of these stories and books in the resources section at the end of this book.

When I read about someone else that has had a dramatic shift in their life, I realize that **I can do it** too. I remind myself that I too can change and bring into my life all that I want.

I have also gone out and done things that have made me inspired. This might include going to trainings or courses or conventions that were related to the things I wanted to do.

For example, I went into management training because I wanted to be a manager. That inspired me to continue to **work hard** and prove to others that I was ready, even though I was young and seemed like the last choice for this sort of role.

Now, what can you do to get and to stay inspired?

## SUPPORT MATTERS

Even though I did a lot on my own to keep my fire stoked and my energy up for my goals, I couldn't have done it without my Bakers and Butlers.

I needed support along the way. I needed someone to remind me that I was a great person; that I would get to where I wanted to go, even when I didn't believe it myself.

Find those people in your life that you can trust to **build you up** when you feel broken down.

You know who these people are. Talk to them when you need the support. Receive their love and support and allow it to energize you and fill you up.

## REWARD YOUR EFFORTS

You can also reward yourself for a job well done when you're changing your life. That seems very appropriate to me.

When you reach certain points or you take certain risks, you may want to take yourself out to dinner or you may want to buy yourself something to **celebrate**.

Whatever you might like to make yourself feel rewarded and special, do it. It works and it makes you feel good.

Plus, if you're not seeing the exact end result you want from your hard work, these rewards can keep you energized until you do see the final results.

It keeps your spirits up and it allows you to pat yourself on the back.

And you deserve it.


## CREATE YOUR OWN PLAN

Right here, think about what you've just read and write down what you will start doing right now. Not tomorrow, not a week from now, and not on a Monday.

Make your plan now.

Take action.

Set your life on fire.

_____

_____

_____

_____

_____

_____

_____

# RESOURCES

Books recommended:
1. *The Holy Bible*
2. *Think and Grow Rich* - Napoleon Hill
3. *7 Habits of Highly Effective People* - Stephen Covey
4. *The Life of an Entrepreneur* - Patrick Bet-David
5. *The 10X Rule* - Grant Cardone
6. *The Secret to Success* - Eric Thomas
7. *Become a Better You* - Joel Osteen
8. *David and Goliath* - David Gladwell
9. *Sell or Be Sold* - Grant Cardone
10. *My Philosophy for Successful Living* - Jim Rohn


Websites Recommended:
1. www.youversion.com
2. www.grantcardoneTV.com
3. www.patrickbetdavid.com
4. www.stephencovey.com
5. www.joelosteen.com
6. www.ETinspires.com

# About the Author:

Louie Herron, a forty two year old entrepreneur, was born In Miami, Florida, in 1974. He is the son of a roofer and father of two children.

Louie has been in the automotive business since he was twenty years old. He started from the bottom as a sales professional, and in fifteen years of experience had his first opportunity of a partnership in a Toyota dealership in Augusta, Georgia in 2006, and two additional dealerships since then (2009 and 2015). He currently operates a Chrysler, Dodge, Jeep, Ram franchise in Madison, GA.

He enjoys the Miami Dolphins (looks to purchase them by age sixty five), and giving motivational/inspirational speeches to youth, college students, churches, civic groups, athletes and other entrepreneurs.

If you would like Louie to speak at your event, church, or school you can send an email to Louieherron@gmail.com or call him at 706-991-1900.